Candle Cra[ft]

A Complete Guide

23 STYLISH PROJECTS & SMALL-BUSINESS TIPS

Tiana Coats

stashBOOKS®

an imprint of C&T Publishing

Text, photography, and artwork copyright © 2023 by Tiana Coats

Publisher: Amy Barrett-Daffin

Creative Director: Gailen Runge

Senior Editor: Roxane Cerda

Editor: Madison Moore

Cover/Book Designer: April Mostek

Production Coordinator: Tim Manibusan

Photography Coordinator: Lauren Herberg

Photography Assistant: Rachel Ackley

Front cover photography by Tiana Coats

Photography by Tiana Coats, unless otherwise noted

Published by Stash Books, an imprint of C&T Publishing, Inc., P.O. Box 1456, Lafayette, CA 94549

Library of Congress Cataloging-in-Publication Data

Names: Coats, Tiana, author.

Title: Candle craft : a complete guide; 23 stylish projects &

small-business tips / Tiana Coats.

Description: Lafayette, CA : Stash Books, [2023] | Summary: "Learn how to

create a variety of candles from poured and molded candles to dipped and

rolled candles. Find out how to select wicks, and work with different

waxes including soy, beeswax, and paraffin. Readers will also learn how

to add in color, scents, and other decorative elements safely"--

Provided by publisher.

Identifiers: LCCN 2022047172 | ISBN 9781644033197 (trade paperback) | ISBN

9781644033203 (ebook)

Subjects: LCSH: Candlemaking.

Classification: LCC TT896.5 .C63 2023 | DDC 745.593/32--dc23/eng/20221013

LC record available at https://lccn.loc.gov/2022047172

Printed in China

10 9 8 7 6 5 4 3 2 1

Contents

INTRODUCTION

Never in a million years did I think I would become a candlemaker. To be honest, I didn't even realize I loved crafting until my late 20s. In 2015, I was working in a cubicle typing in pharmacy prescriptions. I was desperate to change my path in life, and I just started thinking of businesses that would allow me to be my own boss. For some reason, I landed on the idea of making candles. I had never made a candle in my life. I enjoyed going out to buy a new candle every week, so I figured I could try to learn how to make my own.

I dove right in and purchased all the equipment I needed to make candles. Once I started, I knew right away that this is what I wanted to do. I quit my full-time job and found a part-time job that allowed me to work on my candle business during the week. To pay for supplies, I sold used board games online and delivered groceries. Today, candle making is my full-time gig. I specialize in making candles that resemble desserts, but I have experimented with many different forms of candle making over the years.

Whether you are looking to make candles as a fun hobby, to start a candle business, or set off on a new path, this book can help you along the way.

Candle Making Terms

Scent throw: The strength of the fragrance in the candle

Cold scent throw: The strength of a candle's fragrance when it is unlit

Hot scent throw: The strength of a candle's fragrance while it is lit

Fragrance oil retention: The percentage of fragrance that a wax can hold

Melt pool: The melted wax from a lit candle

Burn time: The amount of time it takes to completely burn a candle

Mushrooming: The ball of carbon that builds up on a wick after burning

Soot: The black puffs of smoke that emit from a lit candle

Tunneling: When a candle does not burn all the wax on the sides of a container, resulting in leftover candle wax

Glass adhesion: The way the wax cools against a glass container, resulting in either smooth adhesion or spots where the wax pulls away from the candle

Wick up: Sizing up to a larger wick

Wick down: Sizing down to a smaller wick

Pour temperature: The best temperature for the wax to reduce imperfections when it's poured into the container

TOOLS AND SUPPLIES

The great thing about candle making is that the required tools are easily accessible. I started making candles on my kitchen stove top using an old pot and a pouring pitcher. Before running out to purchase new equipment, take a look around your home to see if you have any of the supplies we're reviewing in this chapter. You're probably going to need to buy a few things, but start with what you have.

Where to Buy Supplies

Start by looking for candle making supplies online. There are many online candle supply shops that have everything you need in one place. I love candlescience.com. They have wax, fragrance, and equipment. I also like to shop at naturesgardencandles.com. They have a wide selection of fragrance oils; if you browse their website long enough, you may find some obscure scents like bacon or fresh cut grass! If you are looking to save a bit of money, you can find gently used equipment on eBay or online candle groups. You can also research local candle suppliers in your area. This is ideal because if you are able to pick up supplies, you can save on shipping.

If you don't have a candle supplier nearby, you can visit a larger craft or hobby store. Usually, these stores have a small candle section with a few wax and wick options. They may also have a nice selection of containers.

Basic Equipment

POURING PITCHER

You need wax pouring pitchers to melt and pour candle wax. Metal is great for retaining heat and keeping the wax hot. I recommend metal pitchers with a plastic handle so you don't need an oven mitt as the pitcher heats up. You can find candle pouring pitchers at almost every candle supplier.

DOUBLE BOILER

Wax is heated in a pouring pitcher with a double boiler. To make a double boiler, you need a pot that is not used for food and a metal pouring pitcher that fits in the pot.

Safely melt the candle wax by filling the pot halfway with water, setting the pitcher in the water, and heating the pot on the stove. Never set a pouring pitcher directly on the stove; this will easily overheat the wax.

PRESTO POT

Presto pots are electric heating pots that are great for melting with temperature consistency. These pots are not necessary, but they do make the candle making process a little easier. You can more easily control your wax temperature with a presto pot, and they hold more wax than a pouring pitcher. You can buy them as is, or you can find altered versions online with spouts. If you go for the spoutless option, use a metal ladle to scoop melted wax from the pot.

THERMOMETER

A thermometer is essential for candle making! You need to monitor the wax temperatures. I personally like to use digital meat thermometers, but you can also use a candy thermometer.

RUBBER SPATULA

Spatulas are great for stirring in fragrance oil. They also come in handy for making dessert-style candles. I recommend getting a completely rubber spatula. The type with wooden handles tend to come apart while you are using them for scooping.

DIGITAL SCALE

You need to precisely weigh ingredients, so I recommend a digital scale.

GLASS MEASURING CONTAINERS

Fragrance oil can corrode some plastics, so it is best to measure fragrance in glass containers. I recommend getting one-cup measuring containers with pour spouts.

WICK HOLDERS

Metal candle wick holders keep the wicks centered as you pour wax. Before I had candle wick holders, I used clothes pins from the dollar store. They work great as well.

WICK TABS/STICKERS OR GLUE DOTS

You will need an adhesive to stick the wicks to the bottom of the candle containers. Wick tabs can be found at almost all candle suppliers. I prefer to use glue dots. Some candle suppliers carry them, but they can also be found on Amazon.

WICK THREADER

This tool is useful to thread wicks through pillar candle molds.

HEAT GUN

Heat guns are great to have to correct any imperfections in the candle wax. I also like to use a heat gun to help clean wax from my tools.

ELECTRIC WHISK

An electric whisk is only needed if you plan on making dessert-style candles with whipped wax topping. Using a hand whisk for this task could work, but it would be very tedious.

BAMBOO SKEWERS

Bamboo skewers help place small details on candles. They come in handy for so many candle projects, and we will use them frequently in this book.

METAL SCRAPER

A metal scraper is handy to have around the workshop. You can use this to clean wax from a surface.

STICKY PUTTY

When working with silicone molds, you need to seal the wick holes with putty to prevent any wax from leaking out of the mold.

Clean Work Space

To keep a clean work station, you need paper towels handy. You can also reuse cardboard you have lying around by laying it on your work surface to reduce cleanup time.

Molds

Candle molds are great because they allow you to create unique candle shapes.

SILICONE MOLDS

Silicone can withstand high temperatures. It is also very flexible, so you can remove cooled wax easily. You can even create your own silicone molds! Look for two-part silicone mold kits at your local craft store.

METAL MOLDS

Metal molds are ideal for making pillar candles (page 61). You may need to use mold release spray, which coats the metal mold with a layer of silicone to make removing wax easier. Search online for silicone mold release spray. Metal molds are inexpensive, and you can find them stocked at most candle suppliers.

VOTIVE MOLDS AND WICK PINS

Votive molds are small molds used to create votive candles. Typically, you will also need wick pins, which act as a placeholder for the wicks as the wax cools.

PLASTIC MOLDS

Plastic molds are another option for pillar candles, and I prefer them to metal molds. I find that plastic molds give candles a shiny finish. Metal molds will easily dent if dropped, and the plastic molds are very durable.

Waxes

Scent Throw

Reminder: Cold scent throw is how strongly the candle smells when not lit. Hot scent throw is how far the scent carries when the candle is lit.

SOY WAX

Soy wax is hydrogenated from soybean oil. Although this wax is very new to the candle making world, it has grown in popularity among candlemakers, mainly because it's biodegradable. This wax typically comes in flake form, and it is very easy to work with. Because it is biodegradable, you can easily clean your candle making equipment in the sink with soap and water.

Soy wax has a melt point of around 113°F to 119°F. This wax is on the harder side, so it melts slower and holds up in hotter temperatures.

Soy wax is notorious for being difficult to scent. The cold scent throw of soy is amazing, but often when you light the candle, the hot scent throw may be hard to detect. It is possible to create a wonderful-smelling soy candle, but it may take quite a bit of testing to nail down the technique.

Soy candles benefit from curing, which means letting the candle sit after pouring and before lighting. Curing a soy candle for anywhere from a week to a month may improve the hot scent throw.

Frosting is more visible in colored soy candles.

Soy wax also commonly frosts, which means a white layer forms on the surface of the wax when the candle cools down in the container. Frosting is not noticeable in undyed candles, but when you add color, you will see the white frosting a lot clearer. This is totally normal, but if you plan to sell the candles, a customer may think that something is wrong. To remedy this, sell soy wax candles with information about the natural frosting process.

You can use soy wax in a variety of ways. Look for soy wax made specifically for your project, including for container candles, pillar candles, and wax melts.

PARAFFIN WAX

Paraffin wax is a byproduct of petroleum and is widely used in candle making. This wax takes scent and color very well. You can use paraffin to make container candles, carved candles, pillars, dipped tapers, and much more. The melting point of paraffin can vary between 119°F and 142°F depending on the type of paraffin wax you are using, so there is a paraffin wax out there that can accommodate a variety of projects. There is also no cure time; they produce a wonderful scent the day after making the candles. I use paraffin wax for the majority of my candles.

Paraffin wax is not biodegradable. Be careful how you discard this wax. Do not empty any wax down your sink, or else you can end up with clogged pipes and an expensive plumbing bill. You can empty any excess wax in a large bucket or container and reuse the wax for other projects. See Recycling Candle Wax and Scraps (page 115) for more ideas on how to reuse your wax.

BEESWAX

Beeswax is harvested from the honeycomb. Bees will cap the cells of the hive with wax. This wax can be removed, and filtered to use for candle making. This is a great option if you are wanting to use natural ingredients to make candles. Beeswax has a higher melting point of around 145°F, so it's best used to make container candles or pillar candles. Beeswax emits a light honey scent, but you can also add additional fragrance or essential oil.

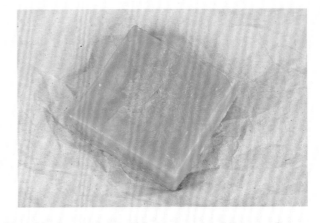

If you are fortunate enough to have access to a beekeeper, then you can get beeswax straight from the source! But you can also buy beeswax online in pellets, blocks, or sheets. Beeswax costs a bit more than other waxes. If you would like to cut down your costs, mix beeswax with soy wax to make your own custom blended wax.

GEL WAX

Gel wax is a transparent candle wax with a rubbery texture. The gel is made from mineral oil and polymer resin. This is a wax to experiment with when you become more advanced with candle making, because it's very different than the other waxes listed here. This wax has a very high melting point of about 225°F, and you can only use zinc core wicks with it. Fragrance oil used with gel wax must have a flash point higher than 170°F, and you can only add ½ ounce of fragrance per pound of wax. Gel wax doesn't retain fragrance oil very well, so it can become flammable if you don't use the appropriate fragrance amount. We'll learn more about fragrance later in this chapter (page 20).

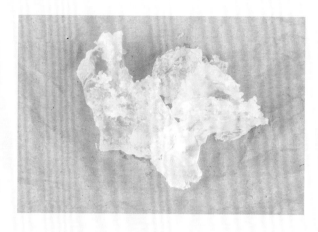

Gel wax is also not known to produce a great scent throw. Many people use gel wax to make highly decorative candles not meant to be burned. You can add nonflammable embeds to the wax such as sand and seashells that will be visible through the transparent wax.

WAX APPLIQUÉ SHEETS

Wax appliqués are great for adding detailed decorations to pillar candles. It is very hard to source these sheets in the United States, so I like to purchase mine from Amazon Germany. These thin wax sheets are easy to work with. You can freehand cut shapes, or you can use cookie cutters for even more design options.

Candle Additives

Additives are compounds that can improve your candle's scent or finish.

STEARIC ACID

Stearic acid helps produce a better scent throw in paraffin wax. It also increases the melting point of the wax. This helps the stability of the candles in hot weather, especially if you are shipping them in the summertime, when they might melt during transport.

VYBAR

Adding vybar to wax can help increase the fragrance oil retention. It can also help to produce more vibrant colors. Usually, waxes that you buy from a supplier already have vybar added, so it's not necessary to add in more. Overusing vybar can restrict the scent throw, so if you want to create your own custom vybar blend, buy wax that doesn't already contain it.

LUSTRE CRYSTALS

Add lustre crystals to the wax to create opaque colors and glossier finishes. I like to use this additive for pillar candles. This is not a common additive, so you may have to do a little searching online to find it.

CANDLE GLOSS

Candle gloss is commonly used when creating carved candles and pillar candles. Use it by dipping a finished candle in a vat of candle gloss, and hanging it to dry. This gloss will create a coating that will give your candle a nice sheen, and it will also protect the candle from debris and fingerprints.

Wicks

Many new candlemakers get a bit intimidated by all the candle wick options on the market, but wicks play an important role in candle making science, so it's important to have options. Different wicks can enhance scent throw, control how fast or slow the wax melts, and reduce the amount of soot that is emitted into the air when the candle burns. Let's run through some of the most common wicks and their uses. We'll review how to choose the right wick on page 24.

Spooled wicks

Wooden wicks

Pretabbed wicks

The first five wick options can be purchased pretabbed. Pretabbed wicks are already primed with a wax coating and attached to a metal tab for ease of use. The wax coating helps the wick stand rigid and also creates a consistent flame.

ECO WICKS

ECO wicks are rigid, flat, braided cotton wicks. They're designed to work best with natural waxes such as soy wax, beeswax, or soy blend wax.

CD WICKS

CD wicks are flat, braided cotton wicks. These wicks can be used in paraffin or in soy wax, and unlike ECO wicks, are considered self-trimming wicks. This means that as the candle burns, the CD wick will begin to curl over, which helps to control the flame. I commonly use these in my own paraffin candles.

LX WICKS

LX wicks are braided cotton wicks designed to reduce soot in paraffin candles. Similar to CD wicks, the LX series is also self-trimming.

Self-Trimming Wicks

Controlling candle flames is an important part of candle safety. Self-trimming wicks are great for keeping a controlled candle flame, but it is still necessary to trim the candle wick before every burn.

ZINC WICKS

Zinc wicks are made from cotton and have a zinc core. These often get confused with lead wicks, which were banned from candle making in 2001. Zinc wicks are safe to use in candle making. The metal core makes the wick rigid, keeping it upright throughout the burn of the candle. The metal in the core also helps to enhance scent throw. These wicks create carbon buildup, called mushrooms, after each burn, which can lead to soot emissions. Trimming the wick before each burn will help reduce and prevent this. These wicks can work in a variety of waxes, and they are the only wicks you should use in a gel candle.

SOOT · *Soot is the black smoke that you see puff up from the candle wick while it is burning. This is caused when the wick forms a mushroom on top or when the wick is longer than ¼˝. Soot can cause damage to walls and furniture by leaving a black coating. It is essential to keep the candle wick trimmed to ¼˝ or discontinue burning a candle at the recommended time.*

SPOOLED WICKS

Spooled wicks are very versatile. Unlike the previous wicks mentioned, spooled wicks are unprimed cotton wicks, which means you can prime them with the wax of your choice. You can also customize the length of the wick, so they're great for tall pillar candles.

If you want to prime spooled wicks yourself, cut the wick down to the desired length, and then let the wick soak in a high–melt-point paraffin or soy wax

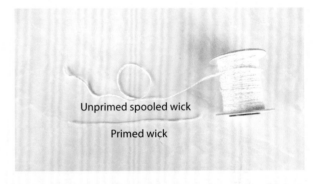

Unprimed spooled wick

Primed wick

for five minutes. After the wicks have soaked, remove them and lay them flat to set. Once the coating has hardened, attach metal wick tabs. You've just made custom wicks!

WOODEN WICKS

Wooden wicks are fairly new to candle making and have grown in popularity for the soothing atmosphere they create. These wicks make a faint crackling sound and produce a larger flame when lit. You can use wooden wicks with any wax. Soy wax and beeswax have a higher melting point, so wooden wicks are a great option for these waxes.

Since wooden wicks produce a larger flame than cotton wicks, it's much easier to accidentally overheat your container. It may take more time to test these wicks to make sure they're safe for your final product. Unlike cotton wicks, wooden wicks are not primed with wax. They use the wax of the candle as fuel to stay lit. If you find that your wooden wick candle doesn't stay lit, you may need to trim the wick shorter so the flame is closer to the wax.

Containers

Choosing a container for your candles is an exciting process. There are many decorative candle containers to choose from, but it is important to make sure you are choosing a vessel that is suited to burn candles.

GLASS

Glass is the most obvious choice when it comes to choosing a candle vessel. Glass is nonporous, and since it's transparent, you can experiment with color and outside-facing designs. The glass needs to be thick enough to hold a flame. Jelly jars and salsa jars are great household options with enough thickness. Stay away from wine glasses or similarly thin containers; thin glass has an increased chance of the glass cracking from the heat. Most candle suppliers carry containers that are safe for candle making, but you can also source candle glass from dollar stores, grocery stores, or craft stores.

METAL TINS

Tins are a great option for candle making. You can use small tins to make travel-size candles or samples. You also don't have to worry as much about imperfections in the design since tins are opaque. Tins do heat up quite a bit, so make sure that you are putting the correct wick in the candle to prevent the tin from getting too hot.

CONCRETE

Concrete containers have grown in popularity. In 2020, supply shortages made it hard for candle businesses to receive their normal stock of glass and tin containers, so many candlemakers started mixing their own concrete and pouring it into silicone molds to create unique candle vessels. It is important to note that all concrete jars need to be sealed with an acrylic concrete sealer. Concrete is porous, so if you skip this step your wax and fragrance will end up seeping into the concrete, which can create dark spots on the vessel.

CERAMIC

Ceramic containers come in a variety of designs and shapes, which means they can be great vessels for unique candles. Ceramic is made from clay and is porous before glazing, so make sure that the ceramic has been glazed before using it for a candle.

Unsafe Containers

It is important to choose safe vessels for candle making. The vessel must be able to withstand the heat of the flame. Thin containers such as wine glasses can burst when exposed to flames. Pie tins are also not ideal for candles because the thin material may overheat and burn the surface it is sitting on.

Fragrance

Scent is one of the most important parts of the experience of burning a candle.

FRAGRANCE OIL

Fragrance oils are a blend of essential, synthetic, and carrier oils. They are manufactured for the purpose of making scented products like soaps, lotions, and candles. Many fragrance oils on the market contain phthalates. Phthalates used in fragrance oils are solvents that help produce more aromatic scents. There is ongoing research on the effects of phthalates in cosmetics and body products. Many candlemakers prefer to opt for phthalate-free fragrance oil. Quite a few of the fragrance oil supply shops online will clearly list if a fragrance has phthalates or not to make it easy for us consumers to make informed choices when shopping for fragrances.

ESSENTIAL OIL

Essential oils are made directly from different plants or herbs, and they can be very pricey compared to other candle scents. Essential oils don't have any carrier additives, so you can expect these candles to produce a very subtle hot scent throw. If you are looking for an all-natural approach to candle making, beeswax and essential oils are a great combo for your candles. We'll review more about essential oil use on page 51.

Pure essential oils are not as stable as fragrance oils. When working with essential oil, it is recommended to use only 6 percent for candle making. For the same reason, add these oils to the wax at a cooler temperature to preserve the scent.

Coloring Candles

Adding color to candles is a simple way to enhance the look of the candle. I like to use color to convey the fragrance of the candle. For example, If I'm using an apple fragrance, I will dye my candles red or green.

LIQUID DYE

Liquid candle dye is great for getting very concentrated colors with a small amount of dye. It can be added directly to melted wax.

DYE BLOCKS

Dye blocks are small wax blocks packed with pigment. Dye blocks are great when you are looking to make a very specific shade. One dye block can make a range of different shades depending on how much wax you melt it with.

TESTING WAX COLORS

The color of the melted wax in the pitcher will be darker than the final color of the solid wax. To test the final color of the wax, drip a small amount of wax onto a paper towel. The wax will cool within a few seconds, and you will see the color the wax will actually be. Then, add more color if you want a darker shade.

ALCOHOL INK

Alcohol ink is not a candle dye, but I like to use it to color the outside of pillar candles. Since this ink is alcohol based, it dries very fast and leaves vibrant pigments. You can apply alcohol ink to your candles with small makeup sponges. We will use this ink in the Marbled Candle project (page 96).

CANDLE SAFETY

Before we dive into making our first candle project, we need to review candle safety. The candle making process requires you to work with flames and high temperatures; staying safe while making and enjoying the candle is the most important part!

Wax Safety

Before you start working with your candle wax of choice, read through the Material Safety Data Sheet (MSDS) for that particular wax. Usually, you will find this information on the website where you purchased the wax, or you can ask the candle supply company to email you the sheet. The MSDS will have important information on how to properly store your wax, how to handle a fire, and the flash point temperature. Most candle suppliers will also list the properties of that particular wax on the website listing. You will find information about how the wax can be used, how much fragrance you can add to the wax, and other important information that may help when creating candles. Remember, candle wax is flammable if it reaches the flash point, so it is very important to know the flash point temperature and make sure your wax always stays below that.

To keep your wax free from debris or moisture, store it in its original packaging. Keep it at room temperature in a dry area. A garage is often not an ideal place to store wax since the temperature fluctuates between seasons.

WAX FIRES

If the wax you're working with ever catches fire, your first instinct may be to grab a cup of water to extinguish the flame, but this will lead to a very dangerous reaction. Candle wax and water do not mix, and this will create a larger flame. Instead, **smother the flame** by putting the appropriate lid on the container or pot. The MSDS sheet will also highlight which type of fire extinguisher to have on hand for that specific wax.

Fragrance Oil

Each fragrance oil also has an MSDS with vital information like flash point temperature. Store oil bottles away from any heat or flames; if your oil comes in contact with an open flame, it may ignite.

Every candle wax has a maximum fragrance load listed as a percentage. For example, most soy waxes will allow you to add a maximum of 12 percent fragrance. Some paraffin wax will only hold a maximum of 6 percent of fragrance. Overloading your wax with fragrance is easy to do. Your first thought for making a stronger-scented candle may be to just add more fragrance. But when you overload the wax, you may experience fragrance oil seepage. This is when your oil starts to leak out of the wax and pool in the candle. If you light a candle with seeping fragrance oil, you could be exposing fragrance oil to an open flame, causing a dangerous fire. We will go over how to calculate fragrance oil load on page 31. It's not as hard it sounds, but it *is* as important as it sounds!

Work with fragrance oil in a well-ventilated room. Make sure pets and children are not in the area, and open up doors and windows. You can also wear a respirator to protect yourself from the vapors.

Candle Testing

Testing your candles is extremely important before handing out candles as gifts, selling them, or burning them for yourself. A successful test will show an evenly burning candle that doesn't overheat the candle container.

Anytime you work with a new wax, wick, container, or additive, you *must* conduct a new test. To stay organized, compile your results in a physical binder or create a digital folder so you can reference the information later. Make sure to record these facts:

- The wicks, fragrance oil, and container material and size used to make the candle

- Fragrance oil percentages

- The exact wax recipe used to make the candle

- The amount of time the candle is lit

- The amount of time it takes the candle to reach a full melt pool

- The amount of soot emitted by the candle (If you suspect the candle is making too much soot, hold a blank piece of paper about 6″ above the candle for a few seconds. If black shows on the paper, the candle is not burning correctly.)

- The scent throw of the candle (Bring others in to smell too!)

- If the candle burns all the wax from the container (This won't be apparent until the candle has burned all the way down. The candle gets hotter as it burns down, so the wax may not begin to burn off the sides of the container until halfway through the burn.)

- The heat of the container (If the container of the burning candle feels similar to touching something straight out of the oven, the candle is burning too hot. Use a laser thermometer to test the candle containers during the burn. They should be around 140°F to 150°F.)

CHOOSING SAFE MATERIALS

The best way to have a successful candle test is to prepare properly before you start candle making.

Choose a wax and container according to the guidelines in the Tools and Supplies chapter (page 7). Then, to choose a wick, measure the diameter of the candle container and look at a candle wick guide. There are many of these guides online, but I recommend using the one at candlescience.com.

In the guide, input the diameter of your container and the type of wax you are using. Considering these two materials, the guide will give a wick suggestion. Whenever I am trying a new wick, I like to purchase the recommended wick as well as one size below and one size above. For example, if the guide recommends an ECO10 wick, I will purchase and test with the ECO8, ECO10, and ECO12 wicks to compare the results. Remember, these resources are only guides, so it is up to the candlemaker to do individual testing.

TESTING THE BURN

For each test, you must burn the candle all the way down, until you have about ½″ of wax left in the container. Burn the candle for four hours at a time, extinguishing the fire and letting the wax cool before lighting again. This may take several days, so stay patient. During each four-hour session, check on the candle to document the behavior of the wick. Beyond recording all the information listed above, you need to determine if the candle is underwicked, overwicked, or just right.

If the candle is underwicked, meaning that the wick is too small for the container/wax combination, you will observe a small flame, and there will be leftover wax on the sides of the container. An underwicked candle may also have a weaker scent throw. If the candle is underwicked, go up one wick size and conduct another test.

Underwicked candle

An overwicked candle, meaning that the wick is too large for the container/wax combination, can be dangerous. An overwicked candle will have a large flame and produce an excess amount of soot. You may also observe that the candle reaches a full melt pool in under one hour.

Overwicked candle

A candle that is properly wicked will do the following:

• Produce a full melt pool between the two- to four-hour marks of your test

• Not produce large amounts of soot

• Have a melt pool no larger than ½″ deep toward the end of the test

• Have a flame no larger than 1″ to 2″ tall

Look for these characteristics to know you have a safely burning candle.

Properly wicked candle

MULTIPLE WICK CONTAINERS

Whenever I am working with a container larger than 4″ in diameter, I like to add three wicks. First, check out the wick guide on candlescience.com. Choose the type of wax you are using, then choose the smallest diameter option for container. I will be wicking the heart-shaped container below for the Triple Wick Candle (page 102). I am using IGI 4630 paraffin wax, and I chose the 2½″ diameter option. According to the CandleScience guide, I should use LX14 wicks for this wax. Next, cut out three circles that are 2½″ in diameter from a scrap piece of paper and mark a dot in the middle of each circle. Place the circles in the container to see how they fit. The circles will represent how big the melt pools will be as the candle burns. The dots represent where you will place the wick in the container.

If you find that the melt pool will not be big enough to melt all the wax in the candle, try increasing the diameter option on the wick guide to make larger circles. This process may take a bit of time, but it will help narrow down potential wick options when testing with larger containers.

TESTING THE SCENT THROW

When I began making candles, I was under the impression that if I just mixed in fragrance, my candle would produce an amazing scent throw when lit. I quickly found out that was not the case. My best friend tried my first candles, and she told me she couldn't smell the candles when she lit them! The experimentation phase is crucial for finding the best scent throw; once safety is covered, play around with different wax, wick, and container combinations to improve scent throw.

Containers and Scent

The wider the container, the more scent the candle will produce when lit. The space you put the candle in will also affect the scent throw. Smaller candles, like single-wick containers around 2½″ in diameter, are better suited for bathrooms and bedrooms. If you want a strong-scented candle in a big space, try experimenting with double wicks in a container that is 3½″ or more in diameter.

STRESS TESTING

Once the wick, wax, and container combination has passed the tests for safety and scent throw, stress test the candle. This means closely monitoring the candle while burning it under different circumstances. Your candle must still be safe when it is put under these conditions:

• Burned longer than the suggested amount of time

• Burned without a trimmed wick

Stress test the candle in a controlled environment. If you notice that the flames get larger than 2″ in height or that large amounts of soot emit from the candle, discontinue the test. Revisit the candle recipe to see if there are any changes that can be made to create a safer-burning candle.

Not every candle user will burn their candles properly. I remember creating what I thought was the perfect double wick candle, but I had only tested this candle under prime conditions. I was shocked when I got an email from a customer saying that the candle jar had cracked while burning. I had burned dozens of these candles in my home without issue, but I wasn't burning them longer than four hours, and I always remembered to trim my wicks. Some candle consumers may ignore this guidance! I immediately reduced the wick size and started using a larger diameter container to prevent the glass from overheating. Stress testing eliminates the possibility of hazard for anyone burning your candles.

Saving Money & Materials

Needless to say, candle making requires an extensive amount of testing. To save some money during the testing phase, pour the wax into an unwicked container. When the wax has hardened, drive a bamboo skewer through the middle of the candle. Then, insert the wick you want to test with upside down. If you start the burn and immediately notice an issue, you can remove and replace the wick in the same container. To remove the wick, blow out the candle and remove the wick with tweezers while the wax is still melted.

Remember that you must complete an entire burn with one wick to fully test the combination of materials, so using one wick at the beginning of a burn and a different wick at the end will still require another complete test burn.

Congrats!
You are now equipped with the knowledge to safely make and test candles.

BASIC CANDLE MAKING TECHNIQUES

Each candle you make will require the techniques in this chapter. Start here, and your candle knowledge will let you create any design you can dream of!

To start, choose a wax, a scent, a wick, and a container. Remember that you need to test your chosen combination before burning regularly.

Weighing Wax

When making candles, it is necessary to measure out the wax by weight. This will help to reduce the amount of waste and ensure you're adding the correct amount of fragrance oil.

To find out how much wax is needed to fill a candle container, set the empty container on a digital scale and tare the scale to zero. Next, pour melted, unscented, and undyed candle wax into the container until the candle container is filled to its final height. Record the wax weight that is on the scale. Now, you will be able to accurately measure out unmelted wax and fragrance for future projects using this container.

To make a batch of multiple candles, weigh out the wax in a metal pouring pitcher. To do this, place the empty pitcher on a digital scale and tare the scale to zero. Now, add the amount of wax needed for the container multiplied by the number of candles you want to make.

Calculating Fragrance Oil Amount

Calculating fragrance oil just takes a little bit of math. Remember that each candle wax has a maximum fragrance load percentage that must be adhered to for a safe burn. Let's start with an example of a quick calculation method used by many candlemakers. This method is not as precise as using something like a specific candle making calculator, but is easy and will not negatively affect the scent throw.

Take a wax with a 9 percent fragrance oil load per 1 pound of wax. First, convert the wax into ounces (1 pound = 16 ounces). Next, multiply 16 ounces, the amount of wax, by 9 percent, the fragrance load (16 x .09 = 1.44 ounces). So 1.44 ounces of fragrance oil is the maximum amount of oil that can be used per pound of wax.

You may notice that the equation above doesn't truly equal 9 percent fragrance oil of the total volume. Once you add the additional volume of the fragrance oil, it's more precisely 8.25 percent. This may bother some makers, but the 0.75 percent difference is miniscule when making candles.

If I'm scenting a large batch of wax or need to be especially precise, I use The Candle Maker Calculator app. This app can help you reduce waste by giving exact calculations for large batches.

Once you know how much oil to use in the wax, weighing out fragrance oil is very similar to weighing out candle wax. Fragrance oil can erode plastics, so weigh out fragrance in a glass container. Place the glass container on the scale, tare the scale to zero, and weigh out the fragrance oil.

Preparing Candle Containers and Wicks

Before pouring wax into a container, you must prepare the container. Use alcohol to spray the inside of the container. Take a lint-free cloth or paper towel and wipe out each container. Doing this will help remove any debris, and it gives the container a clean surface so the wick sticker will adhere to the bottom of the container nicely. Only use alcohol to clean candle containers. Alcohol will evaporate quickly, whereas any other household cleaner may not evaporate from the container, which could make burning dangerous.

Once you have determined the best wick for a project, adhere the wick to the container. There are a few different options available for this task. For a while, I used hot glue; just add a spot of hot glue to the bottom of a wick tab and position the wick in the center of the container. Push down on the wick tab to ensure the wick is firmly in place. If the container opening is too small to fit your hand inside, use a reusable plastic straw to help guide the wick. Insert the wick into the straw, apply the glue, and use the straw to position the wick. Press down firmly on the straw to secure the wick in place.

I decided to move away from hot glue after burning myself too many times. Wick stickers or glue dots are great alternatives. Wick stickers can be found at most candle supply shops, or I usually purchase a bulk box of glue dots on Amazon.

Trimming Candle Wicks

Whenever I talk to customers about candle care, many of them are surprised to learn that there is a proper way to burn a candle. If you flip over any candle from a maker or manufacturer, you may notice care directions. Following these instructions prolongs the life of the candle and helps keep the candle from overheating.

Trimming the wick before each burn is one of the most important parts of safely burning and caring for a candle. To trim a candle wick, extinguish the flame and let the candle rest until it has rehardened. When you're ready to light the candle again, take scissors, nail clippers, or a wick trimmer and cut the wick until it is approximately ¼″ high. I prefer to use wick trimmers because they are designed to cut the wick to the correct height.

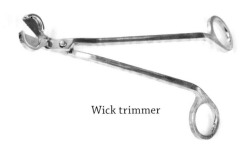

Wick trimmer

Burning Freestanding Candles

Freestanding candles, such as pillar and taper candles, are mainly used for ambiance and decor, as they don't come in a container.

Burning Pillar Candles

Pillar candles don't need to be contained in any way. They are usually created to stand on their own, or in decorative stands made specifically to display these candles. A properly made pillar candle is dripless if burned correctly.

Trim the wick of the pillar candle to ¼″. Light the candle for around three hours or until you notice the wax is about to reach the edges of the candle.

While the candle is still warm, gently push the edges of the candle inward. Doing this will help utilize all the wax from the candle.

Pillar candle after several burns

Heating Wax and Pour Temperature

To heat wax, set up a double boiler on the stove. Fill a pot halfway with water and bring it to a low boil. Set a pitcher filled with the correct amount of wax for the container into the water, and let the wax melt completely. Monitor the wax temperature with a thermometer, making sure the wax doesn't heat over the flash point temperature. If the wax is getting too hot, remove it from the water and reduce the heat.

Melted wax must be poured at a certain temperature. The pouring temperature is not an exact rule, but I have found the temperatures that work best for me based on the wax I'm using, and I will be recommending a pouring temperature to you in each project. Pouring at these specific temperatures can help with glass adhesion and reduce the number of imperfections to fix later.

The ideal pour temperature can be different based on the candle making environment. It is best to make your candles in an area with a stable room temperature, around 65°F. If you make candles in a cold room, you may notice more holes developing in the wax or the wax shrinking away from the glass. If your candles consistently have imperfections, experiment with the pour temperature. Pour the wax at a hotter or cooler temperature to see what works for you and your environment.

Coloring Wax

Adding color to wax is a simple way to enhance the look of your candles. Let's go over the dos and don'ts of coloring candle wax.

Use dye that is specifically made for candle wax. Candle dye comes in block and liquid form. Block dye is a small, highly pigmented block of wax that can be cut up to create a wide range of colors. To use this dye, cut off the desired amount and melt it into the candle wax. Liquid candle dye is great for creating consistent colors. The liquid dye is easy to measure since you can count the amount of drops being added to a recipe. This dye also colors wax instantly. To create more pastel shades with liquid dye, you can dip the tip of a toothpick into the dye and mix it into the wax. See more about dye on page 21.

There are some candle tutorials floating around that may instruct you to use crayons or mica powder to dye your wax. Even though these options may color the candles nicely, they can cause the candle to burn poorly. Crayons and mica powder can clog the wick, causing the candle to produce a very small flame. This can lead to weak scent throw and tunneling. Make sure to use candle-specific dye to achieve the best burn results.

Fixing Imperfections

A couple of hours after pouring candles, you may find that they have developed wet spots against the glass or holes and cracks on the wax surface. Sinkholes develop when air pockets form near the wick. The wet spots you see are from the wax pulling away from the glass in some areas. The pour temperature and the ambient room temperature play a part in both of these issues. You may have to experiment with these temperatures to reduce the amount of imperfections. You can also preheat the containers in a 170°F –190°F oven before pouring the wax. Warming up the containers helps to cool the candles more evenly. Personally, I've found that whenever I warm up my containers I see a drastic improvement in the overall look of the finished container candles.

Don't worry if you do end up with these imperfections. To fix them, remelt the entire top and sides of the candle using a heat gun, making sure to fill the sinkhole or crack with melted wax. Then, let the candle sit for about 30 minutes. This can be time-consuming if you have to do it for every batch of candles. So again, experimenting with your temperatures will save you time in the long run.

Imperfections fixed

CANDLE PROJECTS

Start with these basic candle projects for experience exploring different wax types and wicks, finding fragrance oils you like, and discovering beautiful candle designs.

I recommend wick sizes and maximum fragrance load for each project, but it is still very important to do your own testing to ensure the safety of the candles. Also remember, it's not always necessary to add the maximum amount of fragrance to achieve a great scent throw.

Experimentation is key to creating scented candles!

Soy Container Candles

Soy wax is a popular choice for candlemakers who want to produce biodegradable candles. Soy container candles are a great beginner project! There are many different brands of soy wax, and you can use what works best for you, but I am using Golden Brands 464 soy wax for this project.

Materials

3 glass jelly jars 2½″ diameter (8 ounce)

1 pound, 5 ounces of Golden Brands 464 soy wax

3 ECO10 wicks

3 wick stickers

2 ounces of fragrance oil

3 wick holders

Metal pouring pitcher

Stove pot

Rubber spatula

NOTES ON MATERIALS

After reviewing the wax properties, I noted that the wax's max fragrance load is 12 percent, which comes out to be about 1.9 ounces of fragrance oil per pound of wax. For this lesson, I will be using a 10 percent fragrance load for 21 ounces of wax. So I need 2 ounces of fragrance oil. I'm using Apple Harvest fragrance from CandleScience. I'm using the ECO10 wicks per the wick guide.

Wick Containers

1. Clean out the candle containers with alcohol and a paper towel to make sure they are free of debris. Adhere one wick to the bottom of each container with a wick sticker. *fig A*

Prepare and Pour the Wax

2. Heat soy wax to 180°F in a metal pitcher on a double boiler.

3. Remove the pitcher from the double boiler and add in the fragrance oil. Stir for 30 seconds. *fig B*

4. Allow wax to cool to 145°F by letting it sit. Set out the jars and prepare to fill them.

5. Pour wax into the jars, leaving about a ½″ of space at the top of the container. *fig C*

LEFTOVER WAX · *You may end up with leftover wax. Pour it into a large silicone mold or some other storage container. We will go over how to reuse leftover wax in Recycling Wax and Scraps (page 115).*

6. Center the wicks with a wick stabilizer, and then leave the candles undisturbed for at least two hours before moving them. *fig D*

Finish the Candles

7. Inspect the candles. Fix any sinkholes with a heat gun.

8. Trim the wicks so that ¼″ of wick sticks out of the wax.

Cure Time

Soy wax requires a cure time in order to produce a scent throw when lit. The cure time can be anywhere from three days to one month, depending on the candlemaker. My preferred cure time is five to seven days.

If you would like to experiment with cure time, light one of each of the three candles at three days, two weeks, and one month to see how the scent differs at each stage. Make sure to replicate the test in the same room each time to get consistent results.

Colored Paraffin Candles

Paraffin is widely used for candle making. I love using paraffin wax for decorative candle making because it takes color so well. There are many different brands of paraffin wax, and you can use what works best for you, but I am using IGI 4630 paraffin wax for this project.

Materials

3 glass jelly jars (8 ounce)

1 pound, 5 ounces of IGI 4630 paraffin wax

½ block of red candle dye

Black liquid dye

3 LX14 wicks

3 wick stickers

2 oz. of fragrance oil of your choice

3 wick stabilizers

Metal pouring pitcher

Stove pot

Rubber spatula

Knife

NOTES ON MATERIALS

After reviewing the wax properties, I noted the wax's max fragrance load is 10 percent, which comes out to be about 1.9 ounces of fragrance oil per pound of wax. So for 21 ounces of wax, I need 2 ounces of fragrance oil. I'm using Potpourri scent from Nature's Garden. I'm using the LX14 wicks per the wick guide.

Wick Containers

1. Clean out the candle containers with alcohol and a paper towel to make sure they are free of debris. Adhere one wick to the bottom of each container with a wick sticker. *fig A*

Prepare and Pour the Wax

2. Use an old kitchen knife to slice the wax into smaller pieces to speed up the melting process. *figs B-C*

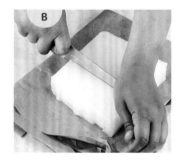

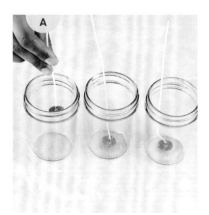

3. Heat the wax in a metal pitcher to 180°F on a double boiler. *fig D*

4. When the wax reaches 180°F, remove the pitcher from the double boiler and add in the fragrance oil. Stir the wax for 30 seconds. *fig E*

Dye the Wax

5. Slice the red dye block into small pieces. *fig F*

6. Add half of the chopped dye pieces into the wax and stir until all the dye is melted.

Fill the First Container

7. Pour wax into the first container, leaving about a ½″ of space at the top of the container. *fig G*

Fill the Second Container

8. Add the remainder of the red candle dye to the pitcher of wax. Stir until all the dye is melted.

9. Pour wax into the second container, leaving about a ½″ of space at the top of the container.

Fill the Third Container

10. Add one drop of black liquid dye to the wax in the pitcher. Stir until the color is completely incorporated. You should see a deep red color. *fig H*

11. Pour wax into the third container, leaving about a ½″ of space at the top of the container.

12. Center the wicks with a wick stabilizer, and then leave the candles undisturbed for at least two hours before moving them. *fig I*

Finish the Candles

13. Inspect the candles. Fix any sinkholes with a heat gun.

14. Trim the wicks so that ¼″ of wick sticks out of the wax.

Paraffin does not require a long cure time. Enjoy the scented paraffin candle the following day.

Beeswax Candles

Beeswax is a wonderful material to use for candles. This wax has a light honey scent, so you can leave them unscented and still enjoy the burning experience. I still like to use a light added scent to my beeswax. Beeswax also has a high melt point, so the wax needs a hot wick to burn. Wooden wicks work great since they tend to produce a larger flame than cotton wicks.

Materials

2 glass containers (10 ounce)

1 pound of beeswax

1 ounce fragrance oil

2 medium wooden wicks

2 wooden wick holders

Metal pouring pitcher

Stove pot

Rubber spatula

Knife

NOTES ON MATERIALS

After reviewing the wax properties, I noted the wax's max fragrance load is 6 percent, which comes out to be about 1 ounce of fragrance oil per pound of wax. So for 16 ounces of wax, I need 1 ounce of fragrance oil. I'm using Honeysuckle from Nature's Garden. I'm using medium wooden wicks according to the wick guide from Lonestar Candle Supply.

Wick Containers

1. Clean out the candle containers with alcohol and a paper towel to make sure they are free of debris. Attach the wick holders to one end of each wooden wick.

2. Place each wick in the center of each container. *fig A*

Prepare and Pour the Wax

3. Use an old kitchen knife to slice the wax into smaller pieces to speed up the melting process.

4. Heat the wax in a metal pitcher on a double boiler.

5. When the wax reaches 165°F, add the fragrance and stir for 20 seconds. *fig B*

6. Let the wax sit. When it cools to 150–155°F, pour the wax into the containers, leaving about ½″ of space at the top of the container. Beeswax sets quickly, so you may notice that the wax will begin to harden on the outside edge of the pouring pitcher. This stage of melt is the best time to pour the wax. Beeswax is a single-pour wax. Try to fill each container completely in one pour. If you try to pour twice, you will see a noticeable line between the pours through the glass container. *fig C*

FINISH THE CANDLES

7. Leave the candles undisturbed for at least two hours before moving them.

8. Inspect the candles. Fix any cracks with a heat gun. *fig D*

9. Trim the wicks so that ¼″ of wick sticks out of the wax.

TRIMMING WOODEN WICKS ·
Cotton wicks are usually primed with candle wax. Priming enables the wicks to stand straighter when cooling, and it also helps the flame to stay consistent while burning. Wooden wicks don't have a wax coating, so it's important to make sure you trim the wick after each burn. The wick needs to use the wax as fuel to keep burning, so keeping the wick trimmed close to the wax is the only way to keep a consistent flame that doesn't go out.

Rolled Beeswax Candles

Beeswax sheets are easy to handle. You can use them to make quick handmade gifts. Kids can also join in on the fun since you don't need to use a hot stove to create these candles. To safely burn the finished candles, either place the candle in a candle holder or on a heat safe plate. Make sure the candle is at no risk of toppling over while burning.

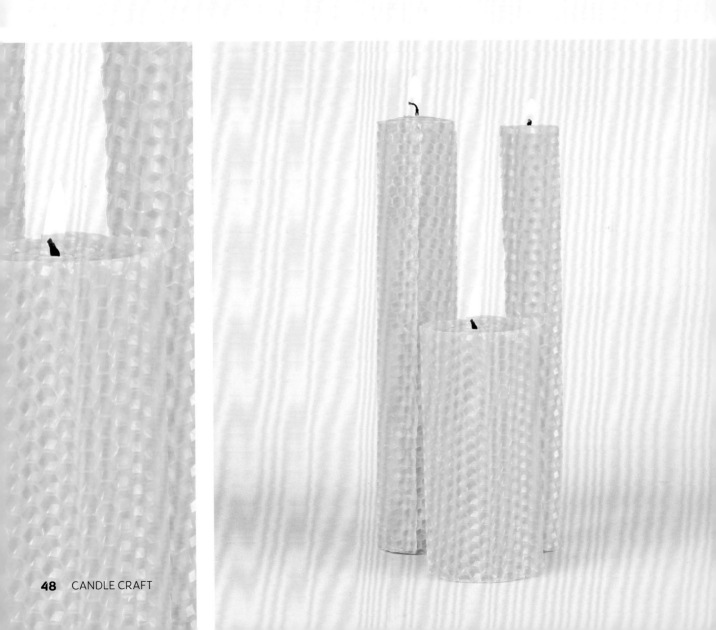

Materials

10 beeswax sheets 16⅓″ × 7⅔″

Spool of #1 wick

Scissors

NOTES ON MATERIALS

Rolled beeswax candles don't need to be melted or scented, so there's not much to worry about in terms of choosing safe materials. Beeswax sheets comes in a variety of sizes and colors. I will be using yellow sheets approximately 16⅓″ × 7⅔″ in size. Each candle will need one sheet. I'm using #1 size spooled wicks to make a stick candle around 1½″ in diameter.

Prepare the Wax Sheet and Wick

1. Lay one sheet of beeswax on the work surface with the short side facing you.

2. Stretch the wick alongside the short side of the wax sheet. Add 2″ of wick length on either side of the sheet, then cut the wick. *fig A*

Roll the Candle

3. Place the wick at the very edge of the short end of the wax sheet, with 2″ of wick hanging past either side. Begin to tightly roll the beeswax around the wick. *fig B*

4. If the wax feels a little too brittle as you roll, use a heat gun to slightly warm up the wax and make it more pliable. Don't melt the wax! Then, continue to tightly roll the beeswax until you reach the end of the sheet. *fig C*

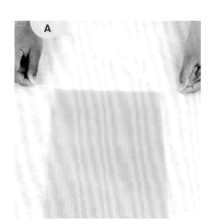

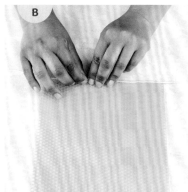

Finish the Candle

5. At the end of the sheet, firmly press the edge of the sheet to the roll to keep the candle neatly wrapped. *fig D*

6. Trim the wick at the bottom of the candle even with the bottom of the wax. Trim the top wick so that ¼″ of wick sticks out of the wax. *figs E-F*

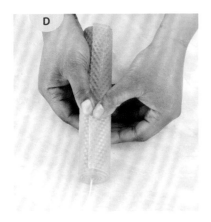

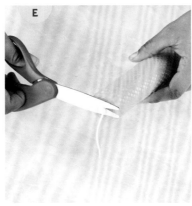

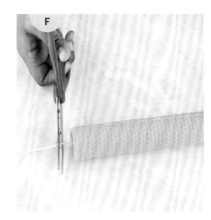

MORE SHAPES • *You can create different sizes of beeswax candles by trimming the sheets in half or using two sheets to roll a large candle. If you make a larger-diameter candle, you may need to use a larger wick to accommodate the size.*

Essential Oil Candles

Essential oils work a bit differently than other scents. Because essential oils do not contain carrier oils, the scent throw is not as strong or as consistent compared to fragrance oils. Essential oils are great if you enjoy subtle scents or want to stick to all-natural materials.

Materials

1 pound coconut soy wax

1 ounce lavender essential oil

4 glass containers (4 ounce)

4 CD8 wicks

Wick holders

Metal pouring pitcher

Spatula

Thermometer

NOTES ON MATERIALS

Use no more than 6 percent of essential oils for candle making since they are not as stable as fragrance oils. I will be using 1 ounce of lavender essential oil per pound of wax.

Wick the Containers

1. Clean out the candle containers to make sure they are free of debris. Adhere one wick to the bottom of each container with a wick sticker.

Prepare and Pour the Wax

2. Heat the wax in a metal pitcher on a double boiler to 150°F.

3. Remove pitcher from the double boiler, then let the wax cool until it reaches 130°F.

4. Add the essential oil to the wax and stir for 30 seconds. *fig A*

5. Pour the wax into each container, leaving about a ½″ of space at the top of each one. *fig B*

6. Straighten the wicks with wick holders.

7. Leave the candles undisturbed for at least two hours before moving them.

Finish the Candle

8. Inspect the candles. Fix any sinkholes with a heat gun.

9. Trim the wicks so that ¼″ of wick sticks out of the wax.

Votive Candles

Votive candles are small candles great for creating an ambient environment on something like an elegant table setting. These candles are typically unscented. To contain the wax, you may want to burn votive candles in a holder or on a heat safe plate.

Materials

1 pound pillar wax

½ blue dye block

10 votive molds

10 votive wick pins

10 LX12 wicks

Metal scraper

Metal pour pitcher

Heat gun

NOTES ON MATERIALS

I'm using LX12 wicks per my wick guide.

Wick Containers

1. Insert one wick pin into each votive container. *fig A*

Prepare and Pour the Wax

2. Heat the wax in a metal pour pitcher to 180°F on a double boiler.

3. Remove the pitcher from the heat and add the dye. Mix the wax until the dye is completely melted.

4. Pour wax into the containers, leaving no space at the top of the container. *fig B*

Finish the Candles

5. Leave the candles undisturbed for at least three hours before moving them.

6. Remove the candles from the votive containers. These containers can have sharp edges so use caution when handling them. *fig C*

7. Flip over each candle and scrape off any excess wax from the wick pin with the metal scraper. *fig D*

8. Hold the bottom of each candle over the heat gun for about five seconds to release the wick pin from the wax.

9. Flip the candle over and tap the top of the wick pin on a hard surface until the candle releases. It's possible that this might damage the surface you're tapping against, so use a scrap piece of wood or another surface you don't mind damaging. *fig E*

10. Place the wicks inside the hole made from the wick pins from the bottom of the candle until the wick tab is flush with the base of the candle. *fig F*

11. Trim the wicks so that ¼″ of wick sticks out of the wax.

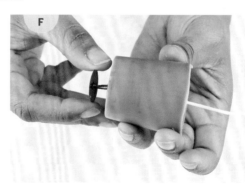

SPECIALTY CANDLE PROJECTS

These specialty candle projects take decor and ambiance to the next level. Scent and burn them regularly, or keep them as beautiful wax sculptures around the home. These projects are formed through molds, dipping, pipping, and more!

Gradient Bubble Candle

The unique look of bubble candles has become very popular online. These candles make for trendy decor pieces, and you can easily experiment with different color combinations. I decided to skip fragrance in this lesson. Fragrance can be pricey, so when making a vibrant and trendy wax sculpture mainly meant for decor, fragrance isn't necessary.

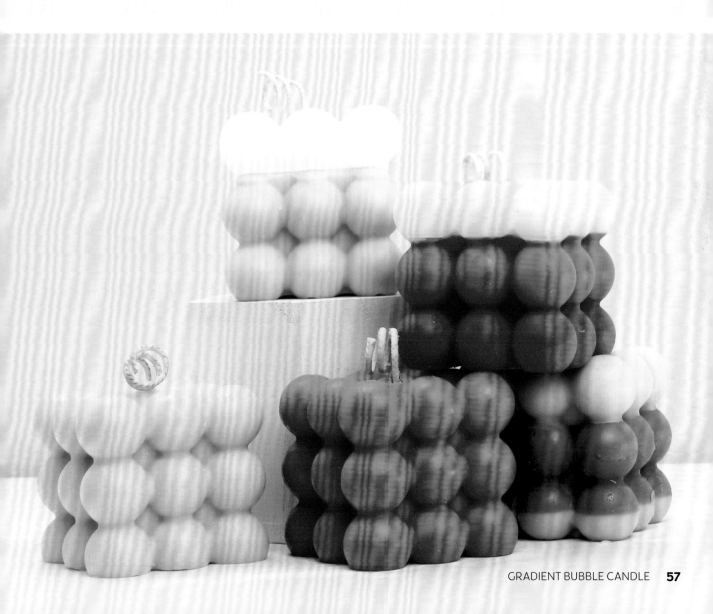

Materials

Square silicone bubble candle mold

8 ounces of soy or paraffin pillar wax

Bamboo skewer

LX20 candle wick

Blue block dye

Putty (optional if bubble mold includes a wick hole)

Metal pouring pitcher

Scissors

Spatula

NOTES ON MATERIALS

I'm using the LX20 wicks per the wick guide. If you are adding fragrance, measure out 10 percent of fragrance or 0.8 ounce for 8 ounces of wax. My bubble mold did not come with a wick hole, but if yours does, follow the first step to prepare the mold. If not, skip that step.

Prepare the Mold

1. Thread the wick through the wick hole in the mold.

2. Plug the hole with putty around the wick.

Prepare the Wax

3. Heat the wax to 180°F in a metal pitcher on a double boiler.

4. If you're choosing to scent the candle, remove the wax from the heat and scent it now.

Pour the Layers

5. Inspect the mold, taking note of where each layer of bubbles ends. To create a clean design, make sure each pour ends where each layer in the mold ends.

6. Cut the blue dye block into small pieces and set aside. *fig A*

7. Pour undyed wax into the first layer of the mold. Allow the wax to set. *fig B*

8. Each layer needs to cool between pours. This will take 30–45 minutes per layer. Turn off the stove during this time. The wax will set in the pour pitcher, but you can easily remelt it when it's time to pour again.

9. If the mold you're using does not have a wick hole, after the first layer is set, add a bamboo skewer into the wax, pointy side down. This technique will allow you to easily thread the wick later on. *fig C*

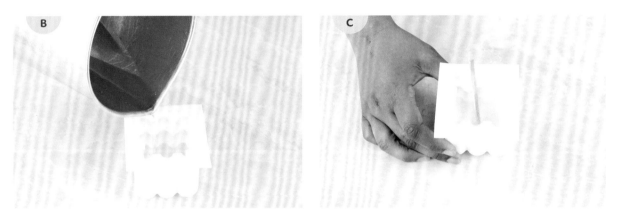

10. Reheat the wax in the pouring pitcher to 180°F. Remove from the heat, then add in a small amount of blue dye to the wax. Stir until the dye is incorporated.

11. Pour in the second layer. Allow the wax to set. *fig D*

12. Reheat the wax in the pouring pitcher to 180°F. Remove from the heat, then add in more blue dye. Make sure to add enough blue dye for this layer to be significantly darker than the previous layer.

13. Pour wax into the last layer.

14. Allow the candle to cool for two hours. *fig E*

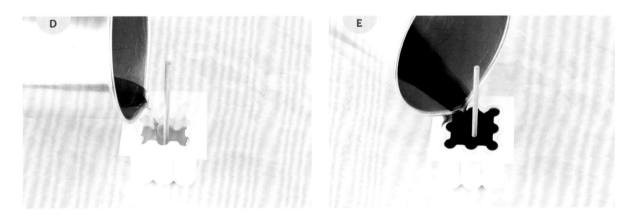

Finish the Candle

15. Carefully unmold the candle by tugging at all four corners of the silicone. Gently flip the sides of the mold down to remove the candle. *fig F*

16. Flip the candle so the white layer is facing upwards and the bamboo skewer is pointing down. Twist the bamboo skewer while pushing upwards to create a hole to thread the wick all the way through the wax. Skip this step if you already threaded the wick through the mold.

17. Thread the wick from the bottom of the candle. *fig G*

18. For a decorative touch, curl the remainder of the wick around the bamboo skewer.

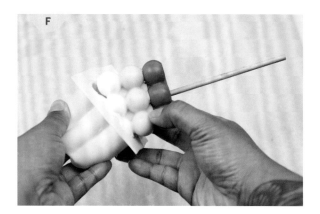

Pillar Candles

Pillar candles are freestanding candles made in a mold. You can add fragrance to these candles, but they don't typically have a strong scent throw, so most of the time I choose to leave them unscented. Pillar wax is formulated to be very hard, so the candle can stand upright while burning. This means the candle will burn slowly, and the melt pool will be smaller compared to a container candle. A smaller melt pool means that the scent throw will be a lot weaker. You can experiment with many different colors and designs. See Flower Appliqués (page 112) for more ways to decorate pillar candles.

Materials

17 ounces of paraffin pillar wax

½ teaspoon of lustre crystals

Purple block dye

Metal pillar candle mold

Spool of #5 wick

2 bamboo skewers

Wick threader

Putty

Rubber band

Scissors

Metal pour pitcher

NOTES ON MATERIALS

I'm choosing to use lustre crystals for these candles because It will make the finished candle more opaque and glossy. I'm using #5 spooled wicks since the diameter of my candle will be 3″.

Prepare the Pillar Mold

1. Measure out the wick to the length of the mold, and then add 2″ of extra wick on either side of the mold. Cut the wick to that length. *fig A*

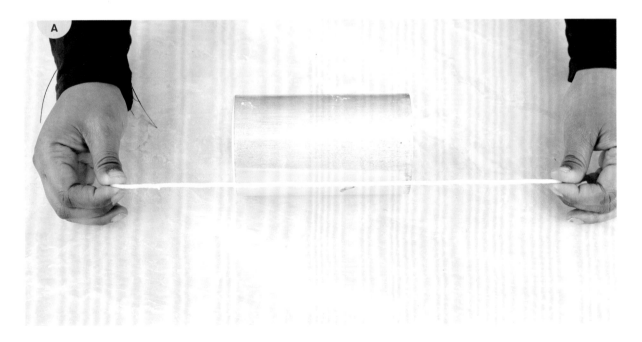

2. Thread the wick through the wick threader, then use the wick threader to thread the wick through the pillar mold. There should be 2˝ sticking out of each end of the mold. *figs B-C*

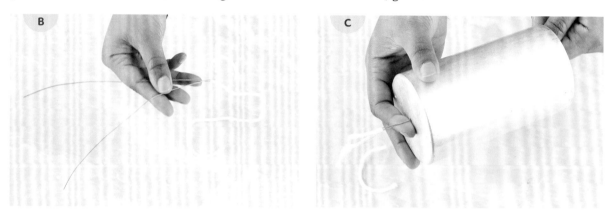

3. Seal the bottom of the mold with putty. *fig D*

4. Place 2 bamboo skewers side by side and wrap them tightly with a rubber band to create a large wick holder. Then, thread the wick at the top of the mold through the skewers to hold the wick upright. *fig E*

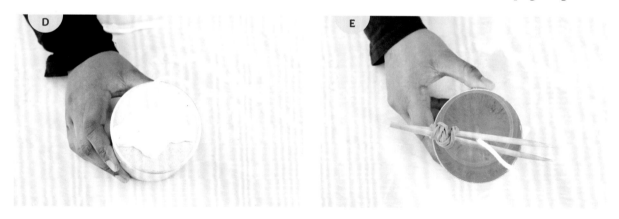

Prepare and Pour the Wax

5. Heat the wax to 180°F in a metal pour pitcher on a double boiler.

6. Remove the wax from the double boiler and add in the lustre crystals. *fig F*

7. Chop up a few small pieces of the dye block, and add them to the wax. Stir until the color is incorporated. I want a pastel color, so I am adding in a small amount. Test the color of the melted wax on a paper towel. *fig G*

8. Once the wax is fully melted, remove it from the double boiler and pour it into the mold. Pour a small amount first to test if the putty has any leaks. Add more putty if necessary. *fig H*

9. Pour more wax into the mold, stopping about ½″ before the top. Save some wax, about 3 ounces, for a second pour later.

10. Let the candle cool for about two hours.

Fill in the Crater

11. You'll notice that a crater appeared in the middle of the candle as it set. Remelt the wax that you saved earlier. *fig I*

12. Pour the wax into the crater of the candle, filling the mold to the brim. *fig J*

13. Allow the candle to cool overnight. The longer it cools, the easier it will be to remove the wax from the mold.

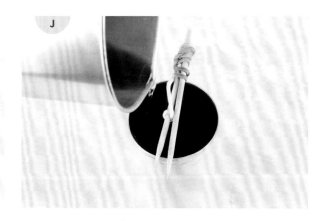

Finish the Candle

14. After sitting overnight, the candle will shrink away from the mold. Remove the putty and skewer.

15. Tip the mold over, and the candle may begin to slide out on its own. If not, gently pull on the wick to release the candle from the mold. Be careful not to pull the wick through the candle. *fig K*

16. Flip the candle over so that the wax that was at the bottom of the mold is now the top of the candle, making the top smoother. Trim the bottom wick flush with the candle and trim the top wick down to ¼".

FLATTEN THE BOTTOM OF THE CANDLE • *If you find that the candle is wobbling while sitting on a flat surface, it might need to be flattened. Place a nonfood cookie sheet on an electric or gas stove on medium heat. Once the sheet heats up, slide the bottom of the pillar candle across the surface a couple of times to melt the candle bottom flat.*

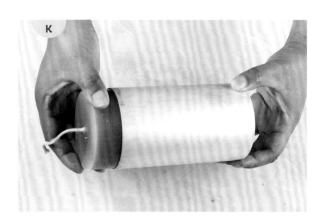

Taper Candles with Mold

Taper candles are perfect for creating ambiance in a space. You can make them in a variety of colors and designs, and they are typically unscented. I love to arrange them in candelabras during the holidays.

Materials

2 ounces of paraffin pillar wax

Green dye block

Wick threader

Spool of #1 wick

Scissors

Plastic taper candle mold

Putty

Bamboo skewer

Metal pour pitcher

Mold release spray (optional)

NOTES ON MATERIALS

Use #1 spooled wicks for taper candles; anything larger will melt the candles very fast.

Prepare the Mold

1. Separate off the top and bottom circle pieces from the main body of the mold. Thread the wick through the wick threader, then use the wick threader to thread the wick through the top piece of the mold. *fig A*

2. Continue threading the wick through the main tapered part of the mold. If you are having trouble guiding the wicking tool through, tie one end to a bamboo skewer and the weight will help guide the wick.

3. Thread the wick through the bottom piece of the mold. Reattach all three pieces of the mold with the wick running through. *fig B*

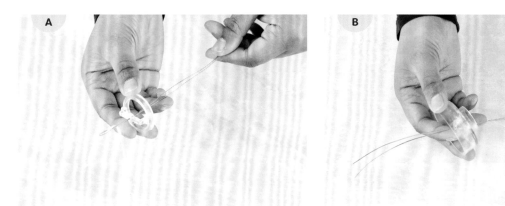

4. Cut the wick, leaving 2″ of excess wick on either end of the mold.

5. Seal both ends of the mold with putty. If using mold release spray, spray the mold at this point. Set aside. *fig C*

Melt and Pour the Wax

6. Weigh out 2 ounces of pillar wax into the pour pitcher.

7. Cut some of the green block dye and add it into the wax. I added a moderate amount for a medium green color.

8. Melt the wax completely on a double boiler, heating it to 180°F.

9. Remove the melted wax from the stove and stir for 30 seconds.

10. Set the mold upright. Pour the wax into the mold, stopping right before you reach the top. Set the remainder of the wax aside for a second pour. Let the wax cool in the mold for 20 minutes. *fig D*

11. After the wax sets, you may see that a crater has formed. Remelt the leftover wax on a double boiler, then fill the crater. Leave the candle to sit in the mold for two hours. *fig E*

Unmold the Candle

12. Remove the putty from both ends of the mold.

13. Remove the top and bottom pieces of the mold. *fig F*

14. Gently rotate and tap the mold on the corner of a table to start to release the candle. If you are having trouble releasing the candle, place the hardened candle in the freezer for five to ten minutes to shrink the wax away from the mold.

15. Pull the bottom wick down gently to fully separate the wax from the mold. Make sure you don't pull the wick out of the candle. *fig G*

16. Trim the top wick to ½″ long and cut the bottom wick flush with the bottom of the candle.

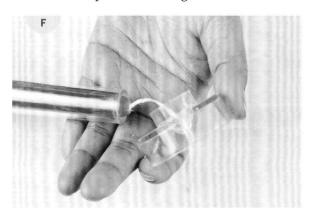

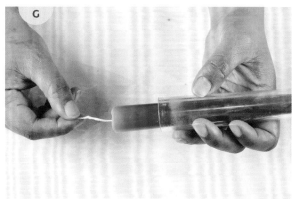

Dipped Taper Candles

Nowadays, we can easily make taper candles with a mold, but for centuries these candles were hand dipped, and there are many candlemakers who still use this technique. I find that although doing it this way may make your arms a bit sore, you can make many taper candles at a time and appreciate the history of this art form.

If you find that a taper candle does not fit perfectly in its holder, insert a piece of sticky putty into the bottom of the holder to help keep the candle upright.

Materials

4 pounds of paraffin cut and curl wax

2 metal pour pitchers 8″ tall

Red dye block

Spool of #1 wick

Scissors

Wooden board approximately 12″ × 2″

4 heavy duty clips

4 metal nuts

NOTES ON MATERIALS

Taper candles are made with #1 spooled wick. Remember that you can always leave wax undyed if that is your preference. The candles will need to hang overnight to set, so you may want to prepare hooks for them to hang on before starting.

Prepare the Wicks

1. Cut two 22″ pieces of wick from the spool.

2. Tie a metal nut to both ends of each wick. The weight of the nuts will help keep the wicks straight while you dip. *fig A*

3. Lift the wooden board and drape both wicks over the board, across the shorter width, with even tails on either side. Position the wicks about 3″ apart and toward the middle of the board.

4. Once the wicks are in place, secure them by clamping them onto the board. Space the wicks so that all four nuts will be able to enter the pitchers.

Melt the Wax

5. Fill up the first pouring pitcher with as much wax as it can fit, and melt on a double boiler. As the wax starts to melt, add more chunks of wax until the pour pitcher is nearly full. Make sure you leave enough room to be able to stir.

6. Chop up the dye block and add pieces to the wax until you reach a desired color. Stir until the color is fully incorporated.

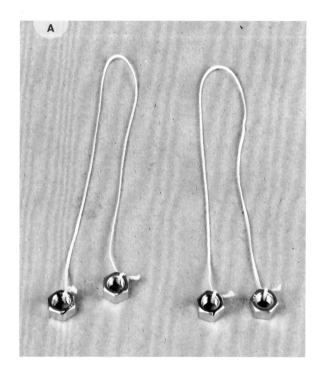

Dip the Candles

7. Remove the wax from the double boiler after making sure the wax is completely melted.

8. Fill up the second pitcher with water and set it next to the pitcher full of wax.

9. Holding the board, slowly dip all four wick ends into the wax, leaving about 1″ of wick space undipped near the board. *fig B*

10. Lift the board, then quickly dip all four of the wicks and wax into the water. *figs C-D*

11. Repeat steps 9 and 10, noticing that the candle will get larger with each dip. I dipped the finished candles for this project approximately 50 times. *fig E*

Finish the Candles

12. After dipping the candles to their desired size, cut off the end of the candle that contains the metal nuts. Remove the nuts from the wax, then toss the wax back into the pour pitcher to reuse later. *fig F*

13. While the wax is still warm, use your hands to straighten the candles if needed. Don't set the candles down on a flat surface. If you lay them flat before they set, the candles will develop a flat spot. *fig G*

14. Remove the clamps, then hang the candles from a hook by their wicks overnight so they can harden.

15. The next day, cut the wicks to ¼″ long.

Longer Candles

The length of the dipped candles is dependent on the length of the wick and the size of the dipping container. To make longer candles, cut your wicks to be up to 10″, then make sure the dipping pitcher is tall enough to accommodate the length of the wick.

Snowy Pine Tree Candle

These pine tree candles are so simple to make. I enjoy using them to decorate around the house, and they make stunning winter gifts.

Materials

Pine tree silicone mold with 2 parts

5–7 large rubber bands

Spool of #1 wick

7 ounces of paraffin pillar wax

0.4 ounce of pine fragrance oil

Metal pour pitcher

Green block dye

Container to hold silicone mold

Scrap paper

Bamboo skewers

NOTES ON MATERIALS

After reviewing the wax properties, I noted the wax's max fragrance load is 6 percent, which comes out to be about 0.9 ounce of fragrance oil per pound of wax. So for 7 ounces of wax, I need 0.4 ounce of fragrance oil. I'm using Fraser Fir scent from CandleScience. I'm using #1 spooled wick since these are small pillar candles. You also need a container to hold the mold steady. Choose a container that is slightly larger than the mold; I'm using a 3″ round cylinder.

Prepare the Mold

1. Stuff the container that will hold the mold ⅔ of the way full with scrap paper. *fig A*

2. Unspool the wick to be the length of the mold, then add 2″ of extra length to either side of the wick and cut.

Decorative Ornaments

One decor option if you don't intend to burn the candle is to use the wick as an ornament hook. Add extra length to the top of the wick so that it sticks out approximately 6″ past the edge of the mold. Then, after finishing the candle, tie the extra-long wick into a loop and hang on the tree.

3. Lay one piece of the mold flat on the work surface with the open side up. Lay the wick in the center of the mold, with 4″ of wick sticking out of the top end. Place the second part of the mold on top. Tightly wrap the mold with rubber bands. *fig B*

4. Place the mold into the container with the hole facing up. Adjust it with the paper to make sure that the mold is standing straight up. *fig C*

Prepare and Pour the Wax

5. Melt the wax in the pour pitcher on a double boiler.

6. When the wax reaches 180°F, add in the fragrance oil. Stir the wax for 30 seconds. Make sure all the wax is melted.

7. Pour the undyed wax into the mold until the mold is completely full. Immediately after, slowly pick up the mold and pour the wax back into the pour pitcher. *figs D-E*

8. Cut up some of the green dye block and add it to the wax. A dark green color will create the best tree, so be sure to test the color on a paper towel to make sure it's the right shade.

9. Once you are satisfied with the color, pour the green dyed wax back into the silicone mold, filling it to the brim.

Center the Wick

10. Attach two bamboo skewers together with a rubber band to create a wick holder.

11. Slide the wick in between the skewers so it stands upright in the middle of the candle. *fig F*

Finish the Candle

12. Allow the candle to cool for two hours without disturbing it.

13. Once the candle is set, remove the rubber bands and separate the mold. *fig G*

14. Trim the bottom wick flush with the candle bottom. Leave the top wick about 2″ long. I recommend handling this candle gently by the wick, as the design can be delicate.

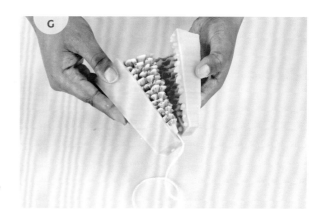

Succulent Garden Candle

Succulents have become a popular home decor plant. This variety of green succulent embeds makes a beautiful soy candle arrangement, and you don't have to worry about watering them! This lovely design can also be repeated with different floral molds and colors.

Materials

Wilton succulent mold

15 ounces of Golden Brands 464 soy wax

1.5 ounces of fragrance oil

Heart-shaped dough bowl or other candle container

3 CD8 wicks

Green block dye

Black liquid dye (optional)

Metal pouring pitcher

Spatula

Heat gun

NOTES ON MATERIALS

After reviewing the wax properties, I noted the wax's max fragrance load is 12 percent, which comes out to be about 1.8 ounces of fragrance oil per pound of wax. I decided to use 10 percent fragrance load. So for 15 ounces of wax, I am using 1.5 ounces of fragrance. I'm using Garden Mint from CandleScience. I determined that the CD8 wicks would be the best fit for this container. See Multiple Wicks (page 27) to see how to triple wick a candle. For my container, I've chosen a heart-shaped wooden dough bowl that holds around 15 ounces of wax.

Make the Succulent Embeds

1. Melt 5 ounces of soy wax in a metal pouring pitcher on a double boiler.

2. When the wax reaches 180°F, add in 0.5 ounce of fragrance oil. Stir the wax for 30 seconds.

3. Chop up the green block dye. *fig A*

4. Add a small amount of green dye to the candle wax. Stir in the dye until the color is incorporated. *fig B*

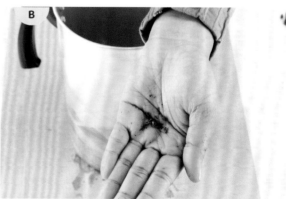

5. Set out the mold. Choose 1–3 shapes of varying shapes and sizes, then fill them with the light green wax. *fig C*

6. Add more of the green dye to the wax to create a medium green. Stir in the dye until the color is incorporated.

7. Choose 1–3 more shapes of varying shapes and sizes, then fill them with the medium green wax. *fig D*

8. Continue to gradually add in more dye to create a gradient of succulent colors. Fill a few molded shapes with each color. If you want to achieve a very dark green color, you can add in a drop of black liquid dye. If you want to lighten the color, add in a little more plain wax.

9. Set the mold aside, allowing the wax to set for one hour.

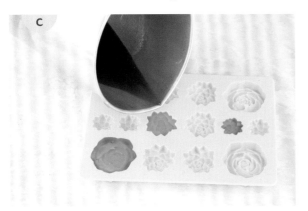

Wick the Container

10. Arrange the 3 wicks in the container in a triangle formation. If you are using a larger or smaller dough bowl, wick the candle accordingly based on the size and shape. *fig E*

Prepare and Pour Wax

11. Heat 10 ounces of wax in a metal pitcher on a double boiler.

12. When the wax reaches 180°F, add in 1 ounce of fragrance oil. Stir the wax for 30 seconds.

13. Pour wax into the container. Set aside and allow the wax to set for two hours. *fig F*

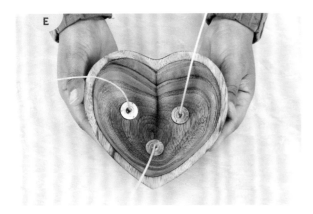

Apply the Embeds

14. Pull the wicks up until they are arranged in the center of the candle. This will be easier to do if the wax is still slightly warm. *fig G*

15. Gently unmold the succulent embeds. *fig H*

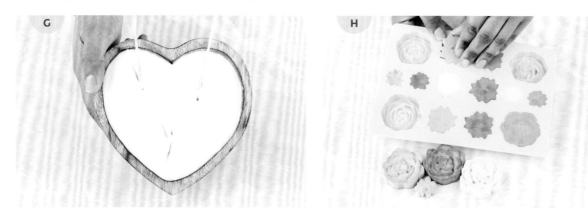

16. Use a heat gun to slightly melt the top of the candle. *fig I*

17. While the wax is still liquid, arrange the succulents on top of the candle in whatever layout looks good to you. Vary the sizes and colors that are next to each other. If not all the embeds fit, store them to use on another project. *fig J*

18. Trim the wicks to about ½″ long, and curl the ends with a bamboo skewer to finish off the candle.

Sand Candles

Sand candles are a great way to make candles quickly. You can also get kids involved in making them without worrying about hot equipment. My candle store has a Sand Candle Bar, and I enjoy watching as children get excited to create their own custom candles. If you have a candle business, this is also a great activity for pop-ups or markets to make your booth interactive. For this project, I'm going to make a fruity blend of sand wax, but you can use any fragrance oil or colors.

Materials

3 pounds of Pillar of Bliss Wax from Nature's Garden

1 ounce of acai fragrance oil

1 ounce of orange fragrance oil

1 ounce of white tea and ginger fragrance oil

Orange liquid candle dye

Burgundy liquid candle dye

Metal or glass mixing bowl

Large square glass container

2 LX18 wicks

Digital scale

Disposable gloves

3 glass containers for storage (1 quart)

Disposable gloves

Disposable spoon

NOTES ON MATERIALS

After reviewing the wax properties, I noted the wax's max fragrance load is 6 percent, which comes out to be about 1 ounce of fragrance oil per pound of wax. There wasn't a wick guide available for sand candles, so I conducted my own test. I determined that the LX14 wick burned well in an eight-ounce jelly jar that is 2.7″ in diameter. I am using a large square container with two LX18 wicks. This wax can also be used to make pillar and taper candles. Glass containers work best with this design, but use any shape for a fun and unique candle.

The wax does not need to be melted to make this candle. The granular nature of the wax helps to distribute the fragrance oil throughout the candle. Make sure to wear disposable gloves any time you touch the wax to prevent skin irritation from the fragrance oil.

Weigh the Wax

1. Tare the scale to zero with a mixing bowl on top.

2. Weigh out 1 pound of wax. *fig A*

Mix the Wax

3. Add 1 ounce of acai fragrance to the wax. Add 4 drops of burgundy liquid dye to the wax. *figs B-C*

4. Put on disposable gloves and mix the wax with your hands until the color is fully incorporated. *fig D*

5. Transfer the mixture to a glass storage container. Do not use plastic containers or wooden bowls. The fragrance oil can corrode plastic and anything porous will absorb the fragrance oil. *fig E*

6. Repeat steps 1–4 with the orange fragrance oil and orange candle dye.

7. Repeat steps 1–4 with the white tea and ginger fragrance oil. I omitted adding in any dye and left the wax white. *fig F*

Form Sand Candles

8. Adhere the wick to the container with a wick sticker.

9. Using a disposable spoon or other scooper not used for food, layer wax into the container. Add wax in any combination to make fun patterns and layers through the glass. Pack the wax into the candle firmly. *fig G*

10. When the container is full, center the wick and trim it to ¼˝.

SHIPPING • *Sand candles don't do well when shipped since the wax can come loose. Instead, consider making and shipping a sand candle kit that recipients can put together at home.*

Watermelon Dessert Container Candle

Learning how to make candles that looked like desserts opened up so many candle design possibilities for me. I really enjoy making these candles because they are different from most candles that you may come across at big-box stores. There are so many unique designs that you can make once you master a few techniques. In this lesson, we will focus on making whipped wax.

Materials

Jelly jar (8 ounce)

10 ounces of paraffin container wax

LX 14 wick

Red block dye

Green block dye

1 ounce of watermelon fragrance oil

Watermelon embeds

Piping bag

Wilton 1M piping tip

Electric whisk

Metal pouring pitcher

NOTES ON MATERIALS

After reviewing the wax properties, I noted the wax's max fragrance load is 10 percent, which comes out to be about 1.6 ounce of fragrance oil per pound of wax. So for 10 ounces of wax, I need 1 ounce of fragrance oil. I'm using Watermelon from Waxy Flower. I'm using an LX14 wick per the wick guide. Glass containers are needed for this design. I purchased the wax watermelon embeds from an Etsy store. If you don't have the appropriate silicone mold on hand, or if you're short on time, there are a large variety of finished embeds available online.

Prepare the Container

1. Adhere the wick to the bottom of the container with a wick sticker.

Melt and Pour the Wax

1. Melt 4 ounces of wax in a metal pouring pitcher on a double boiler.

2. When the wax reaches 180°F, add in 0.4 ounce of fragrance oil. Chop the red dye into small pieces, and add a pinch of dye to the wax. Stir for 30 seconds.

3. Pour all of the wax into the candle container.

4. Let the wax cool for 45 minutes. *fig A*

Make the Whipped Wax

5. Melt 4 ounces of wax in a clean metal pour pitcher on a double boiler.

6. When the wax reaches 180°F, add in 0.4 ounce of fragrance oil. Chop green dye into small pieces, and add of pinch of dye to the wax. Stir for 30 seconds.

7. Let the wax cool down until it becomes cloudy. This may take 15–20 minutes. You can put the wax into a fridge for about 7–10 minutes to speed up this process. If you use the fridge to cool the wax, keep an eye on it. You don't want it to become completely solid.

8. While the wax is cooling, cut the tip of the piping bag and insert the piping tip. Set up the electric whisk.

9. When the wax is ready, whip it with the whisk for about two minutes.

10. When the wax has the texture of whipped cream, transfer it into the piping bag.

Finishing the Candle

11. Adjust the wick to be in the center of the candle. Pipe the wax around the wick so that the wax comes to a point at the top of the candle. So when the wax melts, it will flow down the sides toward the jar. It's okay for the piping to be taller than the container. *fig B*

12. While the wax is still soft, add one watermelon embed to the top of the candle. *fig C*

13. Trim the wick to ¼˝.

Sundae Candle

I really enjoy experimenting with realistic food candles. These candles take time to perfect, but once you get the hang of all the techniques, they can make for amazing decor pieces. Whenever customers come into my candle shop, they are so amazed that these are completely made of wax! If you want to keep these pieces displayed for a long time, make sure to put them in a cabinet where they won't attract dust.

Materials

Glass sundae boat

3 LX14 wicks

1 pound, 10 ounces of paraffin container wax

8 ounces soy container wax

3.5 ounces of vanilla fragrance oil

10 grams of stearic acid

Cookie dough / ice cream scoop

Tray

Banana silicone mold

Cherry silicone mold

Silicone cake pan 6″

Parchment paper

Brown alcohol ink

Paintbrush

Brown liquid candle dye

Yellow liquid candle dye

Red liquid candle dye

Black liquid candle dye

Pink liquid candle dye

Bamboo skewer

Electric whisk

Piping bag

Wilton 1M piping tip

Scissors

Metal pouring pitcher

NOTES ON MATERIALS

This candle will not burn evenly when lit, so it is better as a decorative piece. I am using LX14 wicks for this project because they produce a small flame, so even if I do light it, the candle will not burn quickly. We're adding stearic acid to the wax. This will increase the melt point of the wax and help stop the thinner dessert shapes from breaking. Remember that if you prefer, you can look for completed embeds online instead of forming them all from molds. Parts of this candle are scented, but it's not necessary to scent each piece because some will be too small to have a fragrant impact.

Prepare Container

1. Adhere 3 wicks with wick stickers 1″ apart to the bottom of the sundae container.

Make Embeds

2. Melt 6 ounces of wax and 10 grams of stearic acid in a metal pouring pitcher on a double boiler.

3. When the wax reaches 180°F, add in 0.6 ounce of fragrance oil. Stir for 30 seconds.

4. Dip the tip of a bamboo skewer in the yellow dye to get a little color, then swirl into the melted wax.

5. Place the banana mold on a tray to avoid distorting the mold later in the process. Pour the wax into the banana mold, filling all the shapes. *fig A*

6. Melt 2 ounces of wax in a clean metal pouring pitcher on a double boiler.

7. Add 1 drop of red dye to the wax and mix for 30 seconds.

8. Pour the wax into the cherry mold.

9. Let both embeds cool at room temperature for about 20 minutes. At that point, you should see a shell start to form on top of the wax. When you see this, you can transfer the embeds to the refrigerator to speed up the cooling process.

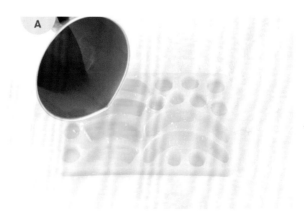

Make Ice Cream Scoops

10. Melt 6 ounces of paraffin wax in a clean metal pour pitcher on a double boiler.

11. When the wax reaches 180°F, add in 0.6 ounce of fragrance. Stir for 30 seconds.

12. Set the cake pan on a tray. Pour 3 ounces, half the wax, into the cake pan. Let wax set for 15–20 minutes. *fig B*

13. Put the pitcher of wax back onto the double boiler until remelted, then add 3 drops of brown candle dye and stir.

14. Pour the 3 ounces of brown wax on top of the white wax in the cake pan. Make sure the white layer is no longer liquid before pouring. Allow the brown wax to set for 15–20 minutes. *fig C*

15. Scoop the wax with the dough scoop. The wax should still be slightly soft, which is the perfect texture to create a realistic scoop. *fig D*

16. Place the scoop on a piece of parchment paper. *fig E*

17. Repeat steps 10–16, dyeing the wax pink instead of brown.

18. Repeat steps 10–16, dyeing the wax yellow instead of brown. *fig F*

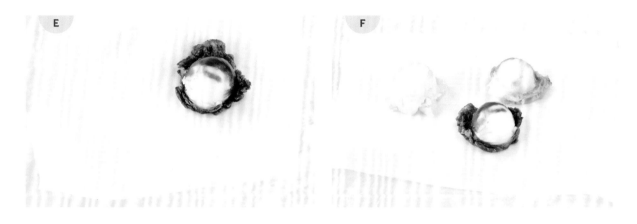

Prepare Embeds

19. Remove the embeds from the fridge. Make sure they are completely set.

20. Remove banana embeds from the mold. *fig G*

21. Place a few drops of brown alcohol ink on a tray.

22. Using a paintbrush and the ink, paint the small banana slices with dots of brown. Leave the larger slices plain yellow. *fig H*

23. Remove the cherry embeds from the mold.

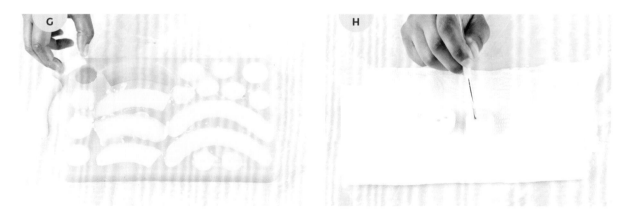

Prepare Whipped Topping

24. Melt the 8 ounces of soy wax in a clean metal pour pitcher on a double boiler.

25. When the wax reaches 180°F, add in 0.8 ounce of fragrance oil.

26. Remove the wax from the double boiler and let it cool for 15–20 minutes until it becomes cloudy.

27. While the wax is cooling, prepare the piping bag. Cut the tip of the bag and insert the piping tip. Set up the electric whisk.

28. When the wax is cloudy, whip it with the electric whisk.

29. Continue to whip for several minutes, until the wax resembles a whipped cream texture. *fig I*

30. Once the wax is ready, move quickly! Scoop the wax into the piping bag.

Assemble the Candle

31. Pipe a few dollops of whipped wax onto the bottom of the container to form a layer of cream. *fig J*

32. Arrange the ice cream scoops on top. If you need the scoops to be placed over a wick, poke a hole through the scoop with a bamboo skewer, and then slide the scoop over the wick. *fig K*

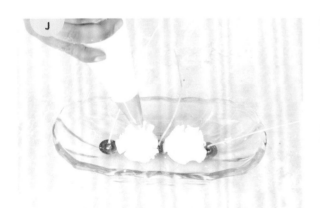

33. Place the bananas on the outside of the scoops with the flat side facing in. *fig L*

34. Fill in any gaps around the shapes with the remaining whipped wax. *fig M*

35. To add a chocolate drizzle, melt a small bit of wax. You will most likely have some leftover wax in one of the pitchers used in earlier steps. Melt the leftover wax on a double boiler.

36. When the wax is melted, add in 2 drops of brown dye and 1 drop of black dye to create a chocolate drizzle.

37. Remove the wax from the double boiler and let cool for about 30 seconds, until it barely starts to thicken.

38. Drizzle the syrup wax onto the sundae.

39. Gently push the cherry embed into the whipped cream dollop to top off the candle. *fig N*

40. Trim or curl the wicks with a bamboo skewer.

Marbled Candle

These candles look complicated, but they are super simple to make. The great thing about this technique is that you don't have much control over the final design. It's always exciting and surprising to see the end result.

Materials

Light-colored pillar candle

2–4 alcohol inks

Parchment paper

Kraft paper

Paper towels

Tray

Disposable gloves

NOTES ON MATERIALS

To make the pillar candle, see Pillar Candles (page 61). This is a design technique to be used on a completed wax candle. This project can get messy. Alcohol inks can stain clothing and surfaces, so make sure to take precautions for cleanliness and safety.

Prepare Surface

1. Prepare your work surface by laying out kraft paper or newspaper. Set the tray on top of the paper, and put on disposable gloves.

Creating the Design

1. Line the tray with parchment paper.

2. Pick out the colors you want to work with. I like to stick with bright colors, because I find that dark colors more often blend together to create muddy shades.

3. On half of the paper, randomly place drops of color. *fig A*

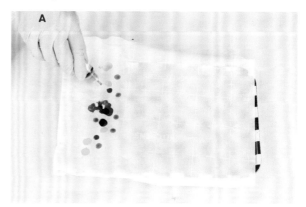

4. Roll the top half of the candle onto the inks until the entire top is colored. *fig B*

5. Lift the candle. If there are any spots with too much color, or if you want to tone down the look, dab the candle with a paper towel. *fig C*

6. Place more colored ink drops on the other half of the paper. *fig D*

7. Roll the bottom of the candle in the ink until it is fully colored. Dab with a paper towel if necessary. *fig E*

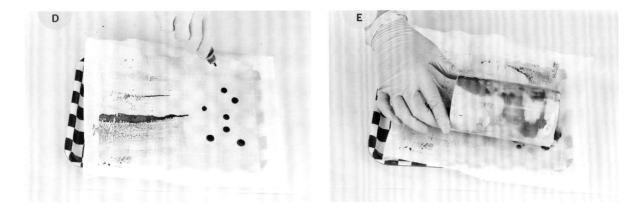

8. If you would like to add more color, add another layer after letting the inks sit for 15–20 minutes. After this time, the inks will have mostly evaporated from the candle. Repeat steps 2–7 as many times as you'd like to complete the design.

9. Let the candle sit for about three hours for the ink to dry completely.

Color Block Candle

These color blocks offer a twist on multicolor candles. This design is a trendy piece of home decor that is super simple to create.

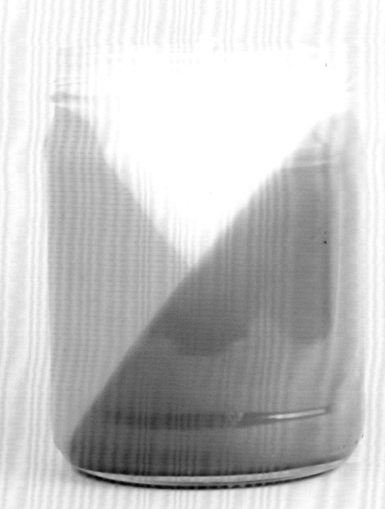

Materials

12 ounces of paraffin container wax

Salsa jar (16 ounce)

LX24 wick

Purple candle dye

Pink candle dye

1 ounce of fragrance oil

2 pour pitchers

Packing tape roll

Digital scale

NOTES ON MATERIALS

After reviewing the wax properties, I noted the wax's max fragrance load is 10 percent, which comes out to be about 1.6 ounces of fragrance oil per pound of wax. I am using 9 percent of the White Tea fragrance from Candlescience. So for this project, I will use 1 ounce of fragrance for 12 ounces of wax. I'm using the LX24 wicks per the wick guide.

Prepare the Container

1. Adhere one wick to the center of the container with a wick sticker.

Melt and Pour the Wax

2. Melt the wax in a metal pour pitcher on a double boiler.

3. When the wax reaches 180°F, add in the fragrance oil. Stir for 30 seconds.

Pour the First Color

4. Place an empty pour pitcher on the scale and tare it to zero. Pour 4 ounces of melted wax into the empty pitcher.

5. Dye the 4 ounces of wax with purple candle dye. Test the color on a paper towel until you reach the desired shade of purple.

6. Lay the roll of packing tape flat on its side. Place the candle container inside the roll, slightly tilting the container.

7. Carefully pour in the purple wax. Let the wax cool for 30–40 minutes until set. *fig A*

Pour the Second Color

8. Remelt the pitcher with undyed wax on a double boiler.

9. Place an empty pour pitcher on the scale and tare it to zero. Pour 4 ounces of melted wax into the empty pitcher.

10. Dye the 4 ounces of wax with pink candle dye. Test the color on a paper towel until you reach the desired shade of pink.

11. Place the candle container inside the roll again, tilting it to the opposite side. The purple wax should be at the top of the container. *fig B*

12. Carefully pour in the pink wax. Let the wax cool for 30–40 minutes until set. *fig C*

Pour in the Third Color

13. Remelt the pitcher with undyed wax on a double boiler.

14. Remove the container from the roll of tape, and sit it upright on the work surface.

15. Pour the undyed wax into the container.

16. Let the candle cool for about an hour before disturbing it. *fig D*

Trim the Wick

17. Once the candle is set, trim the wick to ¼˝.

Piped Triple Wick Candle

The piping doesn't need to be perfect for this design. An imperfect design reminds me of a homemade cake!

Materials

Heart-shaped glass container

3 LX14 wicks

14 ounces of paraffin container wax

1 ounce of cake fragrance oil

Red liquid candle dye

Blue block dye

Bamboo skewer

Metal pouring pitcher

Piping bag

Small open-star piping tip

Scissors

Electric whisk

NOTES ON MATERIALS

After reviewing the wax properties, I noted the wax's max fragrance load is 10 percent, which comes out to be about 1.6 ounces of fragrance oil per pound of wax. I am only scenting 10 ounces of the wax. So I will be using 1 ounce of fragrance for 10 ounces of wax. I'm using Buttercream scent from Nature's Garden. Review Multiple Wicks (page 27) to see how I decided to use LX14 wicks for this project.

Prepare the Container

1. Measure the need for 3 wicks by printing 3 circles with 2½″ diameters. Mark a dot in the center of each circle, and arrange the circles in the bottom of the container.

2. Place the 3 wicks into the container using the wick guides. *fig A*

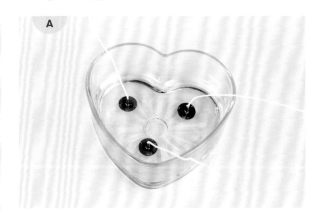

Melt and Pour the Wax

3. Melt 10 ounces of paraffin wax in a metal pour pitcher on a double boiler.

4. When the wax reaches 180°F, add in the fragrance oil.

5. Dip the tip of a bamboo skewer in red liquid dye to pick up some color, then stir it into the wax until the color is incorporated.

6. Pour the wax into the glass container. *fig B*

7. Let the candle cool for two hours.

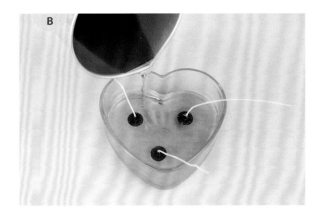

Piping

8. Melt 4 ounces of paraffin wax in a clean metal pour pitcher on a double boiler.

9. Chop up a block of blue dye into small pieces. Add a pinch of dye to the melted wax. Test the dye on a paper towel until you achieve the desired color.

10. Remove the wax from the double boiler and let it cool until the wax becomes cloudy. You can put the wax into a fridge for about 7–10 minutes to speed up this process.

11. While the wax is cooling, cut the tip of the piping bag and insert the piping tip. Set up the electric whisk.

12. When the wax is ready, whip it with the whisk.

13. When the wax has the texture of whipped cream, transfer it into the piping bag.

14. Pipe a border around the candle. *fig C*

Cake Slice Candle

You can make very realistic pastries with wax. These cake candles are best used as decoration; if you burn this candle, it will tunnel down the middle of the wax. The fragrance in these sweet decorations will become more fragrant over time.

Materials

16 ounces of soy pillar wax

Candle wick

Raspberry embed mold

Red liquid candle dye

Brown liquid candle dye

Closed-star piping tip

Piping bag

Scissors

Spatula

1.6 ounces of fragrance oil

Cake slice silicone mold that holds 6 ounces of wax

Bamboo skewer

2 candle pouring pitchers

Disposable fork or electric whisk for whipping

NOTES ON MATERIALS

Since I won't be burning this candle, I can use any wick. I've chosen LX12. After reviewing the wax properties, I noted the wax's max fragrance load is 10 percent, which comes out to be about 1.6 ounces of fragrance oil per pound of wax. I'm using Black Raspberry Vanilla scent from Nature's Garden. Allow this soy wax candle to cure for 5–7 days for the best scent throw results.

Melt the Wax

1. Melt the wax in a metal pour pitcher on a double boiler.

2. When the wax reaches 180°F, add in the fragrance oil. Stir for 30 seconds.

Prepare the Wax

3. Pour 6 ounces of melted wax into a second pouring pitcher.

4. Add 2 drops of brown liquid dye to the pitcher and stir until the dye is incorporated.

5. Pour the brown wax into the cake slice molds. Let it cool for 20–30 minutes. Clean out the pouring pitcher. *fig A*

6. Pour 6 ounces of melted wax into the second pouring pitcher.

7. Add in 3 drops of red liquid dye and stir until the dye is incorporated.

8. Pour some of the red candle wax into the raspberry mold. Set aside the rest of the wax to cool. This will be the red mousse of the cake slice. *fig B*

9. You should have 4 ounces of wax left in the first pouring pitcher. Set this pitcher aside to cool. This will be the whipped cream topping.

Top the Candle

10. Set up the electric whisk. Whip the red wax until it has a texture similar to thick cream. *figs C-D*

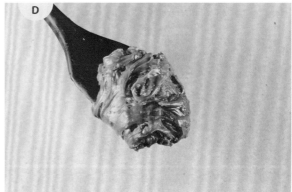

11. Spread the pink wax frosting onto the brown cake base as you would a cake. *fig E*

12. Add a bamboo skewer pointy side down to the center of each slice as a placeholder for the wicks. Allow to sit for an hour. *fig F*

13. Carefully remove the cake slice from the mold. Slowly push the bamboo skewer into the slice until you see the skewer pierce the bottom of the candle. Remove the skewer and replace with a wick. Cut or curl the wick. *fig G*

14. Remelt the white wax and whip it up until it is a whipped cream texture.

15. Cut the end of the piping bag and insert the piping tip. Spoon the cream into the piping bag.

16. Pipe two dollops of cream onto the cake slice. *fig H*

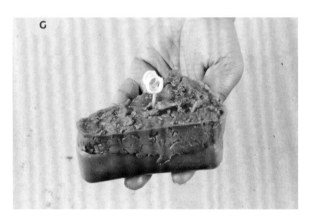

Finish the Candle

17. Unmold the raspberry embeds. Top each dollop with an embed. *fig I*

18. Allow to set for two hours.

Latte Candle

These latte candles are so relaxing and cozy! In this project, we will be learning how to create a delicious two tone drink candle.

Materials

12 ounces of soy container wax

Candle wick

Wick stickers

Wick stabilizers

Glass mug (16 ounce)

Red liquid candle dye

1 ounce of strawberry milkshake fragrance oil

Scissors

Bamboo skewer

Disposable fork or electric whisk for whipping

2 metal pouring pitchers

Paper towel

Heat gun

NOTES ON MATERIALS

Measure the diameter of the container being used, and reference a wick guide to determine the wick you need for this project. I've chosen ECO16. After reviewing the wax properties, I noted the wax's max fragrance load is 12 percent, which comes out to be about 1.44 ounces of fragrance oil per pound of wax. I have decided to use 9 percent fragrance load. So for 12 ounces of wax, I will use 1 ounce of fragrance oil. I'm using Strawberry Milkshake from Bulk Apothecary. Allow the finished soy candle to cure for 5–7 days to enhance the scent throw.

6. Allow both pitchers of wax to cool to around 120°F.

7. Once the wax has reached 120°F, use the electric whisk to whip the wax until it reaches a thick consistency similar to heavy cream. You want to be able to pour the wax into the mug, so you do not want to over whip it to whipped cream texture. If you do over whip it, place the wax back on the double boiler to remelt it.

8. Once the wax has thickened to a heavy cream consistency, pour the white wax into the mug. *fig B*

Wick the Glass Mug

1. Attach the wick(s) to the bottom of the glass mug using wick stickers. *fig A*

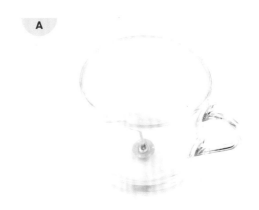

Melt the Wax

2. Melt 12 ounces of wax in one metal pour pitcher on a double boiler.

3. When the wax reaches 180°F, add in the fragrance oil. Stir for 30 seconds.

Prepare the Wax

4. Pour 6 ounces of melted wax into the second metal pour pitcher to separate the wax.

5. Add 1 drop of red liquid dye to one of the pitchers and stir until the dye is incorporated. Do not add dye to the second pitcher.

9. Immediately pour the red wax on top. *fig C*

10. Quickly, begin to blend the two colors together inside the mug with a bamboo skewer. Where the two colors meet, press the bamboo skewer against the glass and create swirling motions. Repeat this swirling motion around the whole container. This will help to get rid of the harsh line and create a realistic latte swirl. *fig D*

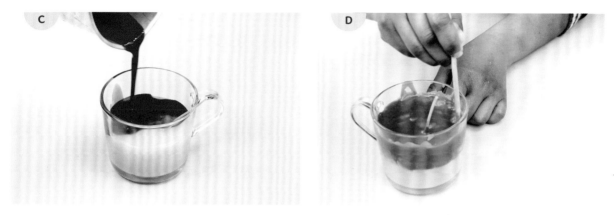

Finish the Candle

11. The candle may have a lumpy top after making the swirl. Clean the edges of the container with a paper towel. Take a heat gun and even out the top of the candle. *figs E-F*

12. Trim the wick to ¼˝ or wrap the wick around a bamboo skewer to curl the wick.

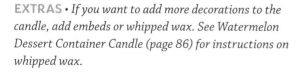

EXTRAS • *If you want to add more decorations to the candle, add embeds or whipped wax. See Watermelon Dessert Container Candle (page 86) for instructions on whipped wax.*

Flower Appliqués

Wax appliqués can be used to turn any simple candle into a fun piece of art. Experiment with adding them to any of the projects in this book.

Materials

Wachsplatten appliqué wax sheets

Flower plunger cutters

Circle plunger cutters

Taper candle

Bamboo skewer

NOTES ON MATERIALS

These appliqué sheets are easy to work with. You can use different-shaped plunger cutters to create unique designs. You can also layer the appliqués to add depth and color. The appliqués may fall off if you plan to ship the candles. To set the design in place, you can dip the finished candle in candle gloss. Hang the candle to dry overnight and the gloss will protect the design.

Cut Out Flowers and Centers

1. Choose a wax color for the flowers. Most plunger sets come with multiple sizes. Cut out different size flowers with the cutters. *fig A*

2. Choose a different wax color for the centers. Cut out different size center circles to fit the sizes of the cut flowers. *fig B*

Place Flowers on the Candle

3. Choose a candle for the flowers to decorate.

4. Place the flowers on the candle. If you are having trouble getting the flowers to stick to the wax, apply pressure to the edges of the flowers so they will stay in place. *fig C*

5. Place the circles in the center of each flower. If you're having trouble handling the small circles, use a bamboo skewer to handle them. Gently press the pointy end of the skewer into the wax to easily pick it up. *fig D*

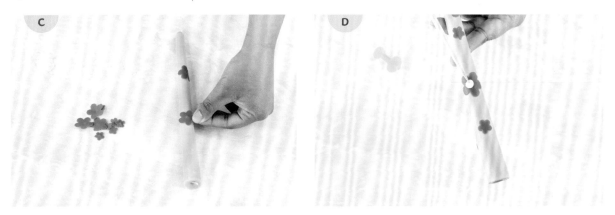

Finish the Candle

6. Make sure all the appliqués are adhered to the candle.

Container Appliqués

You can also use appliqués for container candles. Repeat the same steps to cut the appliqués and apply them on the inside of the container. Make sure the appliqués are pressed firmly against the glass, and pour the wax into the container.

RECYCLING CANDLE WAX

You may often end up with extra wax after you finish a project or after some projects that might not turn out how you wanted them to. The ideas in this chapter will help you to use up all those extras so no scrap is wasted!

Tealights

Tealights are small candles great for creating ambient lighting. Since these candles are very small, they don't put off a strong scent throw. They also burn quickly, and the containers can get hot. To protect furniture and prevent accidents, burn these in a tealight holder.

Materials

Tealight containers

Tealight wicks

Recycled candle wax

NOTES ON MATERIALS

Make sure you have a general idea of the wax's qualities before heating the scraps so that you can do so safely. You can use mason jars or any other decorative holder meant for tea lights for these containers.

Wick the Containers

1. Adhere the wicks to the containers with a wick sticker. I like to wick a whole bag of tealights in advance so I will always have some ready in case I have extra wax I need to recycle.

Pour the Candles

2. Heat the leftover wax scraps in a metal pour pitcher on a double boiler.

3. Pour the wax, filling each tealight container. *fig A*

4. Let the candles sit undisturbed for at least two hours.

Outdoor Bucket Candles

Bucket candles can be great additions to an outdoor function. They can be made from any mix of waxes.

Materials

Galvanized bucket

Spool of #6 wick

Wooden wick tabs

Wick stickers

17 ounces of recycled candle wax

2 bamboo skewers

Rubber band

Metal pour pitcher

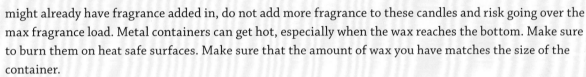

NOTES ON MATERIALS

Since bucket candles are larger and will be made from wax that might already have fragrance added in, do not add more fragrance to these candles and risk going over the max fragrance load. Metal containers can get hot, especially when the wax reaches the bottom. Make sure to burn them on heat safe surfaces. Make sure that the amount of wax you have matches the size of the container.

If you don't like the idea of blending all of the scents from your scraps together, separate your extra wax into scent categories as you work. Have one container for citrus scents, one for bakery scents, and so forth.

Wick the Containers

1. Measure out enough wick for the length of your container and add 2˝. Cut the wick. Repeat this step to make two wicks.

2. Thread each wick through the wick tab. I find it easier to use wooden wick tabs to secure larger wicks. *fig A*

3. Attach the wicks to the bottom of the bucket with wick stickers. *fig B*

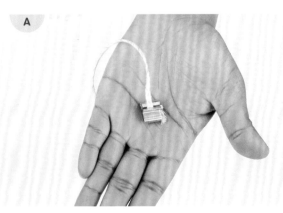

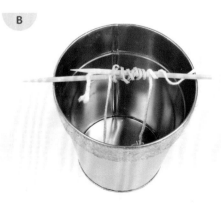

Melt the Wax

4. Chop up the wax scraps into small pieces and add them to the metal pour pitcher. *fig C*

5. Melt the wax on a double boiler.

Pour the Wax

6. When the wax is completely melted, pour it into the bucket.

7. Wrap 2 bamboo skewers together with a rubber band. Slip the wick through the skewers to keep it centered and set it on the top of the bucket. If the skewers are too short, stagger them to make them sit on top of the bucket. *fig D*

Trim the Wick

8. Once the candle has set for two hours, remove the skewers and trim the wick to ¼″.

SELLING CANDLES

Candle making can be a fun hobby, but if you're anything like me, you will eventually end up with more candles than you can burn! You may even start to get comments from friends and family telling you to start selling your candles.

I have been running my handmade candle business, Winding Wick Candles, for many years, and I have some tips to help guide you if you are looking to start your own candle business.

Before You Start Selling

FIND YOUR WHY

Before starting your business, determine your "why." Why are you starting this business? Do you want to become the next big candle retailer? Do you want to sell on the weekends at your local farmer's market? Or are you in it just to make some extra cash? The beauty of a small business is you can keep your business small or work to grow it larger. Either way, you should have an idea in mind of what you hope to do.

The candle business isn't a get-rich-quick idea. It takes time to grow your business, and you have to be okay with not making much profit in the first few years. I didn't start profiting from my candle business for three years, but I enjoyed creating and learning about business, so I stayed consistent and kept working. Take time to really think about your "why" before moving forward. Starting a business is a big commitment!

TESTING CANDLES

If you decide to sell candles, testing them first becomes even more important! **Testing is an absolute must** before selling your first candle. At the time of writing this book, there aren't many regulations, so it is up to the candlemaker to make sure they are delivering a safe product to their customers. Read more in Candle Testing (page 24).

BUSINESS INSURANCE

Another necessity is insurance. I have had many new candlemakers express that they are not able to afford product liability insurance in the beginning stages of their business, and they ask if it is truly necessary. The truth is that **insurance is a necessity for any business**. Candles are an open flame in the home. I'm sure you hate to imagine anything going wrong with your candles, but it is possible that your candle could be part of a fire or accident. It is important to protect yourself and your

assets. Get your candle insurance no matter how small your business is!

TAXES

Taxes are a part of every business. Check with a tax professional to get more information on how you should be handling business taxes. It is also important to set up a separate business account to keep your personal and business finances separate. Quickbooks.com is also a great tool to help keep track of your business expenses. I really like using this program to track receipts, and it is easy to view your profit and loss at glance.

DETERMINE A BUDGET

You'll need to look into all the materials and tools necessary for getting your candle business up and running. At this stage, it is best to sit down and create a budget. There are tons of fancy containers, printed boxes, and packaging materials that you can purchase to really make your brand stand out, but it's important to make sure you are not going overboard before you get started.

This can also help you determine how much you are going to charge for your product. If you want your candle to be in the $20 range, then you have to make sure the materials you are buying will allow enough profit to make that work. When pricing my products I like to multiply my cost by four. So if the candle cost me $3 to make, then I will sell it for $12. Your pricing formula may change as your business grows, but I find that multiplying the cost by four to start is a good way to make sure you are making enough profit from your products.

Use Spreadsheets

It can be pretty difficult to look at one finished product and think about how much the wax, fragrance, wick, and container costs for that individual candle. Use a spreadsheet to start tracking the cost of the materials. This will give you a good idea of how much you need to set aside for your materials, and it will help with determining your retail price. There are many sellers on Etsy that create spreadsheets specifically for handmade makers that I find useful.

DIY BRANDING

DIYing many parts of my business in the beginning helped me keep my costs low. Thankfully, we live in an age where so much information is free and easily accessible. I definitely didn't have the money for custom stickers or branded packing material when I started, so instead I learned how to piece together my own versions. I am not much of a 2D artist, so I turned to Etsy to purchase commercial images from sellers that I could use on my candle labels.

I hand cut my candle stickers for about a year before I had money to invest in a Cricut machine. I still use my Cricut instead of ordering stickers from a third party. You can also buy blank precut labels from an office goods store and print your own designs on them.

Photography is also an important business skill. If you are looking to start posting on social media or selling online, then you will need attractive photos to capture the attention of your buyers. It took me a couple of years before I realized that my photos weren't doing my candles justice. I started watching YouTube videos on how to use cameras and lighting, and I learned a bit about photo editing. Enlisting the help of a photographer from time to time may be necessary, but learning to take your own product photos will save you a lot of money and bring in lots of new customers.

FIND YOUR NICHE

While you're in the product development stage, start thinking about your niche. Who do you want your brand to appeal to? Is your candle brand going to be luxury, minimal, quirky, retro? This is where you can really get your creative juices flowing. I recommend creating a brand board for your business

and compiling images and color palettes that represent the overall aesthetic for your brand.

It is important to establish a niche for your product so that you can find an ideal audience, and your buyers will also have a clear understanding of what you're selling. Figuring this out in the product development stage also helps you save money. For example, If you have no idea who you are marketing to you or what your look should be, you could find yourself buying many different containers, waxes, and packaging materials only to realize down the line that those items don't fit with your brand.

DO TRADEMARK RESEARCH

Naming your business might be the hardest part of developing a brand. You want something easy to remember that is also unique. So think about the niche you picked out and see if you can think of a name that ties everything together. Create a brainstormed list.

Try to include the word "candle" somewhere in your business name. It will help significantly when it comes to online search engines. It is also very important to make sure you are not infringing on an existing trademark. It doesn't matter how small your business is; protect it from any future problems. Visit uspto.com to search your potential business name and see if it's available. You also want to make sure you are able to acquire the website domain and social media accounts for the name.

BUSINESS PLAN

At this point, you have a good idea of what you want your business to look like, but you need to think about the direction you want your business to go. Writing a business plan will help you determine where you need to be spending your valuable time. I have to admit, I didn't have a business plan until years into my business. Learn from my mistakes! A business plan will make it a lot easier for you to make business decisions. A business plan doesn't have to be complex. You need to at least have an idea of your niche, description of what your company offers, target market, the product, competitors, budget, marketing strategy, and goals along with the timeline to achieve these goals. There are many free resources online that can help you write out a business plan.

Selling at Local Markets

BENEFITS OF IN-PERSON SELLING

So you've got your candle recipe down, your business plan made, and now you're ready to sell your first candles! Selling face-to-face allows you to get direct feedback, and you get to practice your sales pitch. Personally, I love selling to customers in person. The whole experience is a lot more friendly, and I find that talking with customers helps to create more word-of-mouth referrals.

QUESTIONS TO ASK THE EVENT COORDINATOR

Before paying for booth space at a market, you want to ask questions so you can determine if the event will be beneficial to your business. Ask the event coordinator about the demographics of attendees and amount of foot traffic at the event. It would be wise to make sure there aren't too many candle vendors already attending. If it's a smaller event, I like to make sure that there is only one other candle vendor besides myself. I once attended an event where there were five candle booths in a small conference room! Needless to say, I didn't get many sales that weekend.

SETTING UP YOUR BOOTH

Setting up your booth can be a little stressful because there are many items you will need to take along with your products. The look of your booth is also important. When setting up your table, try to add vertical dimension to your display. Set your products on risers or crates to make everything look more interesting than they would flat on the table.

Make signs that show your prices; people may shy away if the prices are not displayed. You also want to engage customers with a good sale. Make it known that your items are on sale for the show only. They may feel more inclined to buy now so they don't miss out on the deal. It is essential to have a credit card reader at events. There are many card reader options, but I personally like using the Square card reader. It is easy to use and set up with my phone.

Customers really enjoy an interactive booth. Remember the sand candles we made earlier in the book (page 82)? This would be a great addition to your setup. Customers will be able to make their own candle within a few minutes. Whenever they burn their candle at home, they will remember the experience of making it at your booth! This is a great way to make a lasting impression with your customers.

BEST PRACTICES

• Be an expert when it comes to your products.

• Make sure you know your USPs (unique selling points). For example, I like to tell my customers that the candles may look like food but everything is wax and handmade in the United States. I also point out that my candles are long lasting and have an excellent scent throw.

• End each customer interaction by giving them a business card. Even if someone doesn't buy from you now, they may follow you on social media and make a purchase later on.

• Meet other sellers. Whenever I go to local events, I like to take a moment to step away from my booth to interact with other businesses. I have met so many amazing business owners just by browsing their products and introducing myself. I always like to meet other entrepreneurs because you never know where that interaction could lead you or what you might learn.

Selling Online

When you combine email marketing and social media with an online shop, you can dramatically increase your customer base. Starting an online shop for the first time may seem intimidating, and there is a lot to learn, but it is totally worth it for your business.

ONLINE MARKETPLACES

If you are a fairly new business and you don't have thousands of people searching specifically for you, marketplace platforms can get new eyes on your products.

The most popular marketplace for handmade sellers is Etsy. Setting up an Etsy store is very simple. You can get a shop up and running within 30 minutes at a low cost. This platform has a built-in customer base of millions of people. Another platform that you can utilize for your handmade crafts is Amazon Handmade. Many people don't even know that this exists, but it blends in seamlessly with the rest of Amazon. You can sign up for an artisan account, and after Amazon vets your application, you can set up a storefront.

All online marketplace platforms take a percentage of each sale. Make sure to evaluate which fees make sense for your business. Amazon is a little pricier than Etsy but has a larger audience base, so it can be worth the extra cost. With Amazon FBA (fulfillment by Amazon), I can also utilize their warehouse by sending in my candles and letting Amazon pack and ship orders. This saves me a ton of time, and I don't have to increase staff to fulfill orders.

Marketplaces like these are awesome to reach new clients, but most customers on these platforms aren't loyal to your brand. They may only remember that they just got your product on Etsy or Amazon, so it can be hard to get returning customers from these platforms.

START YOUR OWN WEBSITE

If you are looking to create your own website to drive traffic and customize the customer shopping experience, then there are a few options that I can recommend. Personally, I like using Shopify to host my website. The interface is easy to use, and there are a lot of options for customization with the Shopify app section. You can also host your own website through Squarespace or Wix. Browse around all the different options to get an idea of the cost and interface. Switching from one platform to another can be a bit of a hassle, so take some time to do your research before you start. These platforms will likely charge lower fees than Etsy or Amazon.

RUNNING AN ONLINE SHOP

Product Photos

Once you've chosen your platform, think about the customer experience on your website. Product photos can make or break a sale. You don't need fancy equipment to take a nice photo. You also don't need to over stylize a photo to capture a customer's attention. Make sure your photos are clear, simple, and free of clutter. If you don't have the budget for photography lights, use sunlight to capture great photos.

Business Email

Start a business email address. This will help you appear more professional, and you won't have all your personal and business emails flooding into one inbox.

Choosing a Site Layout

You want to make a customer's shopping experience easy to navigate. Less is more! The more work customers need to do to buy a product on your site, the more chances there are for them to abandon their cart during the process. Visit established websites in your niche and see how their website is laid out. Take notes and apply some of those concepts to your own website.

DRIVING CUSTOMERS TO YOUR SHOP

After you've spent time creating your website, you need to drive traffic there to make sales. This is the hardest part of having an online shop. There are so many competitors online, so you need to think about how you can get people to choose you. Your niche is a big part of this; the branding on your website needs to be cohesive, and you need to have a good idea of who you are marketing to.

To get your target audience to your online listings, familiarize yourself with search engine optimization (SEO). Essentially, SEO means using certain keywords to target your ideal shopper. You need to find out what your demographic is searching for. For example, there are many small candle businesses that are in the niche of making literary candles. This means they are going to create candles based on scents of their customer's favorites books and characters. If someone was searching for an Alice in Wonderland–themed candle, they may search for words like wonderland, red queen, or Lewis Carroll. So it's good SEO practice to associate your products with those relevant terms.

Remember to not infringe on trademarks on your products or in your product listings. It is very possible to create items geared toward a fan base without using copyright terms. You just have to use a little creativity with the names!

Using Social Media

CHOOSING A PLATFORM

Almost every small business with an online shop is on social media. Social media is a great way to market your business for free, but it can be very overwhelming to create content. My advice with social media is to go slow and steady. Choose a platform that you enjoy posting to consistently. My favorite place to post is on YouTube. I really enjoy the creative process for making videos, but there is a lot of work that goes on behind the scenes that other people may not enjoy as much. If you don't see yourself posting long-form content on YouTube, try out platforms that emphasize short-form content like TikTok or Instagram.

When you first start your social media account, don't feel discouraged if you aren't growing as fast as you like. Keep posting consistently, stay true to your niche, and your audience will eventually start to find you. If you have a lot of content available, new people can look at the backlog of your work and get inspired. So if your content isn't getting seen today, don't stress about it. New people discover my YouTube channel every day, and they watch videos I posted years ago.

SHARING YOUR STORY

My last piece of advice is to share your story. People don't want to just see your products; they want to connect with you. Small businesses have the opportunity to interact with their customer base at a personal level. You can tell your story by making videos about how your brand started, showing behind the scenes of your business, introducing your team, and going live and chatting with your audience. Share the "why" you started with! Make a connection, and people will begin to resonate with you and your products.

ABOUT THE AUTHOR

Tiana Coats began her candle making journey in 2015, when she decided she wanted to pursue a creative career path. She noticed that there weren't many creative candle designs on the market, so she set out to create a company that would offer unique scented candles.

After months of testing different waxes, wicks, and scents, Tiana started Winding Wick Candles in the spring of 2015. A few months later, she left her office job for a part-time weekend job so she could dedicate more time to growing her business.

Tiana made Winding Wick Candles her full-time career in 2020. Over the years, Tiana has grown a YouTube channel, been featured in major publications, launched a successful candle making business course, and has recently opened her first retail candle shop in her hometown. Now, she's compiling all of her candle making knowledge into this book so that others can enjoy the art of candle making. She lives in Ferris, Texas.

FIND HER ONLINE AT WINDINGWICKCANDLES.COM.

CREATIVE SPARK

ONLINE LEARNING

Crafty courses to become an expert maker...

From their studio to yours, Creative Spark instructors are teaching you how to create and become a master of your craft. So not only do you get a look inside their creative space, you also get to be a part of engaging courses that would typically be a one or multi-day workshop from the comfort of your home.

Creative Spark is not your one-size-fits-all online learning experience. We welcome you to be who you are, share, create, and belong.

Scan for a gift from us!